WEAPONS
FOR WARRIORS

BLOOMER

Bookmark
PUBLISHING
DALLAS, TEXAS

WEAPONS FOR WARRIORS

Published by Bookmark Publishing, Dallas, TX.

Copyright © 2012 Bookmark Publishing.
Copyright © 2001 by George Bloomer, The School of Ministry Series.

Unless otherwise noted, all Scripture quotations are taken from the Holy Bible, King James Version.

ISBN: 1-59024-477-X

Printed in the United States of America

10 9 8 7 6 5 4 3 2 1

Contents

Lesson 1:   Satan, You're Not a Sovereign......11

Lesson 2:   The Plot to Destroy Destiny..........29

Lesson 3:   Satan's Fall and Holy War...........47

Lesson 4:   Knowing Your Adversary.............65

Lesson 5:   Demonology and Government......81

Lesson 6:   Devices of Satan.......................111

Lesson 7:   Oppression, Depression,

Possession 133

Lesson 8:   How To Cast Out Demons 151

Lesson 9:   Phases of Demonology..............171

Lesson 10: What is Witchcraft?...................193

Lesson 11: Religious Demons 221

Lesson 12: Identifying and Breaking Generational

Curses...................................247

Lesson 13: How to Reject Rejection 259

Lesson 14: Addiction................................275

Lesson 15: The Spirit of Pride 287

Lesson 16: The Power of Worship 303

Lesson 17: Angels Among Us 317

Lesson 18: From Atom to Adam 343

Introduction
So, you think you know warfare?

Did you know that a stronghold can live in you throughout your Christian life; and do you really understand what it means to wage spiritual warfare against the enemy?

Satan is real, and in order to combat and have victory over his deadly forces, we must activate the faith and power freely given to us by the Father. Furthermore, we must expel every false doctrine and teaching that comes to distract us from God's truth.

Many myths on how to defeat the enemy have infiltrated the Body of Christ, watering down the Word of God and preventing the saints from operating in God's glorious power. In this technological age of quick fixes and quick results— from seven steps to salvation, to the three steps of casting out demons—we've attempted to fight the evil forces of the enemy through manmade methods, when the Word of God clearly states that *the weapons of our warfare are not carnal, but mighty through God to the pulling down of strongholds* (1 Cor. 10:4). Lucifer's plan is to stop you, and he doesn't care how he does it. Disguising himself as an angel of Light, the devil comes only to steal, kill, and ultimately destroy you (John 10:10)!

For years and years, the Body of Christ has been deceived into thinking that the battle is over after salvation. We've been taught to speak clichés instead of speaking the Word of God; to make excuses rather than confronting real issues; to operate in the fear of man instead of revering God, and to talk about what the devil is doing instead of taking the appropriate action based on God's Word to defeat every satanic attack.

Throughout the New Testament, Jesus Christ was confronted with oppositions from demons and we, likewise, will be confronted with and forced to pull down the enemy's strongholds. Many Christians make statements like, "The devil is attacking my finances, my home," and so forth; and they never experience the victory, simply because they do not understand the concept of spiritual warfare. Since the beginning of the Charismatic movement, there has been limited teaching in the church regarding pulling down strongholds, breaking generational curses, or exposing Satan through some of his worst forms: intimidation, manipulation, and domination. This is why it's important to recognize God's truths verses Satan's counterfeits.

For instance, no other form of satanic attack has been stronger or more violent, as it relates to spiritual warfare, than the attack that Satan has launched through drugs and sexual perversion. Satan is very subtle in camouflaging his purpose, gripping the mind to accelerate his destruction. Our society today is very aware of the drug population on the street, but Satan has blinded the minds of mankind in medical science. The doctors would much rather prescribe the same drugs used on the street (but under a different name) to alter the mental faculties of mankind. Consequently, there are just as many drug users under medical supervision as there are on the streets; but because individuals are under medical supervision, it then becomes less likely for the natural mind to recognize and discern Satan's subtle attacks.

Strongholds cannot be properly destroyed with pills. The only lasting relief comes through the power of God. This is why the devil is so strongly opposed to the deliverance ministry. Just as God draws from the **praises** of His people, Satan and his demons draw from the **suffering** of God's people.

Throughout the Word of God, it is revealed how Satan uses his tactics to frustrate the purpose of God's people. For example, in Ezra chapter four, the people of God encountered adversaries in the process of building God a house. Satan's entire purpose is to *frustrate the purpose* (Ezra 4:5) of God in the life of the believer; *but the Lord, Himself, frustrates the tokens of liars and drives the diviners mad* (Isaiah 44:25). We have power as believers to abhor and inhibit the works of darkness, thereby causing them to go back to their source.

The Lord has placed a call on my life to expose witchcraft and the subtleties of Satan throughout the world as well as minister to those within my local congregation. Having authored the book, *Witchcraft In The Pews*, which reveals how witchcraft affects Americans in our society and the church, I have been brought into a deep study of God's Word concerning spiritual warfare and how we have accepted many of Satan's deceptions without question.

It is important for believers who thought they knew about spiritual warfare to understand that Satan wants to darken our understanding, so that constant exposure to the Word will have little or no effect. Make no mistake about this truth; we **are** engaged in spiritual warfare.

This is no weak, watered-down teaching, but a teaching that will reveal to you who Jesus really is, enable you to discern His presence, and equip you with the weapons needed to engage in spiritual warfare against the adversary. The lessons of our spiritual warfare class will emphasize thought-provoking truths designed to expose the subtleties of Satan, thereby, enabling you to engage in spiritual warfare and destroy the works of the enemy.

Many believers do not want to consider the reality of spiritual warfare. This is why, all too often, believers find themselves fighting on a carnal plain— person against person.

In this in-depth study, you will learn about strongholds and how to defeat the enemy; how to engage in spiritual warfare through the simplicity of the Word of God; and how to become equipped for warfare as never before.

Prepare to find out how much you really know about spiritual warfare and dispel the myths once and for all!

—Bishop George G. Bloomer

LESSON

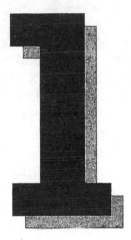

SATAN, YOU'RE NOT A SOVEREIGN

To the only wise God our Savior, be glory and majesty, dominion, and power, both now and ever. Amen.
—Jude 25

INTRODUCTION

When we begin to compare the power of Satan to that of God's, the contrasts are very significant. Although Satan may have caused the fall of the human race as the serpent, he is not sovereign, though he refuses to admit his limitations.

Remember that Satan is a deceiver. So many believers tend to believe that Satan has more power than God has, but of course, this is not true. In the lesson, "The Plot to Destroy Destiny," we will see that although Satan retains his intelligence, wisdom, and power, after his fall, his power does not and can not exceed the power of Almighty God. Although Satan has knowledge and wisdom, he is the greatest fool of all. His wisdom is not true wisdom. His plan is to make you believe that he is something that he is not. He is under divine control and can not do anything outside of God's permissive will.

Psalms 103:19 reveals the position that God has prepared for Himself in the heavens. *The Lord hath prepared his throne in the heavens; and his kingdom ruleth over all.*

Prayer

Lord Jesus,

We worship and praise You as Lord of all. All creation is because of You, and should continuously praise You for Your wondrous works and love. We pray that this lesson would open our eyes to Your true power. May we truly know at the end of this lesson, how much power we really walk in through Christ Jesus. Make us bold, confrontational soldiers for Your glory. In Jesus' name. Amen.

LESSON

In II Chronicles 6:14, Solomon expressed the sovereignty of God during his prayer of dedication by these words:

> *And said, O Lord God of Israel there is no God like thee in the heaven, nor in the earth; which keepest covenant and showest mercy unto thy servants that walk before thee with all their hearts.*

The sovereignty of God reveals Him as the supreme *ruler and lawgiver* of the entire universe. He is the King over all the earth.

It is important to note the contrasts on the following chart the sovereignty of God versus the non-sovereignty of Satan.

GOD IS...	SATAN IS...
1. God is Infinite.	Satan is finite.
2. God is Omnipresent.	Satan is not.
3. God is Omniscient.	Satan is not.
4. God is Omnipotent (has **all** power).	Satan is not. Satan has **limited** supernatural power.
5. God is All-Loving.	Satan does not care, but breeds on hate and power.
6. God is Truth.	Satan is a Liar.
7. God is Faithful.	Satan is a Deceiver.

ELIJAH EXPOSES
THE SOVEREIGNTY OF GOD

Sovereignty: 1. supreme excellence or an example of it   2. a) supreme power esp. over a body politic   b) freedom from external control: AUTONOMY   c) controlling influence 3. one that is sovereign; esp.: an autonomous state

There are many relevant Bible stories, which prove the sovereignty of God versus the non-sovereignty of Satan, such as Satan's role in the story of Job, and the story of how Satan was given power to give life to the beast in the book of Revelation. In the story of Elijah versus the prophets of Baal (another name for Satan), a duel takes place further proving God's unlimited power and Satan's predestined defeat:

> *[18]And he answered, I have not troubled Israel; but thou, and thy father's house, in that ye have forsaken the commandments of the LORD, and thou hast followed Baalim.*
> *[19]Now therefore send, and gather to me all Israel unto mount Carmel, and the prophets of Baal four hundred and fifty, and the prophets of the groves four hundred, that eat at Jezebel's table.*
>
> —1 Kings 18:18-19

King Ahab had been searching for the prophet Elijah to possibly slay him (1 Kings 18:10). He finally met Elijah in verse 19, and said to him, "Oh, you're the one causing all the trouble in my kingdom" (for there was a famine in the land; and Elijah had previously prophesied to King Ahab that there would be no rain for several years). To which Elijah responded, "No, you're the one troubling your kingdom because of your worship to Baal, thus for- saking the commandments of the LORD." So in an effort to prove to the king that the worship of Baal was a sin, and also to prove the power of

Jehovah God, Elijah challenged him to a spiritual duel. He called for 450 of Baal's prophets, and for 400 prophets of the grove to help him prove his point.

> [21] *And Elijah came unto all the people, and said, How long halt ye between two opinions? if the LORD be God, follow him: but if Baal, then follow him. And the people answered him not a word.*
> [22] *Then said Elijah unto the people, I, even I only, remain a prophet of the LORD; but Baal's prophets are four hundred and fifty men.*
> [23] *Let them therefore give us two bullocks; and let them choose one bullock for themselves, and cut it in pieces, and lay it on the wood, and put no fire under; and I will dress the other bullock, and lay it on wood, and put no fire under:*
> [24] *And call ye on the name of your gods, and I will call on the name of the LORD; and the God that answereth by fire, let him be God. And all the people answered and said, It is well spoken.*
>
> —1 Kings 18:21-24

So there are 850 people opposed to Elijah, who believe that Baal is the only god. In any person's mind, one would probably think that Elijah was absolutely insane to go up against 850 people, but he was confident in the Lord God Almighty. He addressed all the people of the kingdom, saying, "Now, it's time for you to decide who you're going to serve. Stop going back and forth. Do you choose to worship God or Baal?" But there was no response, so he then gave the prophets the challenge. He dared them to prepare a sacrifice and then call on their gods to answer by fire. He would do the same; and whichever God answered by fire would be declared **the** True and Living God.

[25] And Elijah said unto the prophets of Baal, Choose you one bullock for yourselves, and dress it first; for ye are many; and call on the name of your gods, but put no fire under.

[26] And they took the bullock which was given them, and they dressed it, and called on the name of Baal from morning even until noon, saying, O Baal, hear us. But there was no voice, nor any that answered. And they leaped upon the altar which was made.

[27] And it came to pass at noon, that Elijah mocked them, and said, Cry aloud: for he is a god; either he is talking, or he is pursuing, or he is in a journey, or peradventure he sleepeth, and must be awaked.

[28] And they cried aloud, and cut themselves after their manner with knives and lancets, till the blood gushed out upon them.

[29] And it came to pass, when midday was past, and they prophesied until the time of the offering of the evening sacrifice, that

there was neither voice, nor any to answer,
nor any that regarded.

—1 Kings 18:25-29

So they did as they were asked, and called upon the name of their god from morning until noon, but there was no response. Their next attempt in contacting their god was to jump on the altar. Elijah mocked them, saying, "Maybe your god is busy. He's probably talking to someone, or on a business trip; or perhaps he's sleeping. Why don't you cry out louder?" So, they foolishly began to cry, and scream, and wail before their god, but there still was no response. They became so desperate that they cut themselves with knives and lancets, till blood was gushing from their bodies. It must have been a sight! Finally, they tried prophesying (obviously not by the Spirit of God) until the evening sacrifice, but still there was no sign of fire from their god.

[30]And Elijah said unto all the people,
Come near unto me. And all the people
came near unto him. And he repaired
the altar of the LORD that was broken
down.   —1 Kings 18:30

Because Satan's power is limited and, in this case, was of none effect, in their own might, the false prophets tore down the Lord's altar in order to prove a point, that they might be glorified and their god. Much like those who seek to steal God's glory today, they tear down that which is holy, forcing the servants of God to go behind them to restore and revert attention back to God and rebuild that which negligently was torn down.

> [31] *And Elijah took twelve stones according to the number of the tribes of the sons of Jacob, unto whom the word of the LORD came, saying, Israel shall be thy name.*
> [32] *And with the stones he built an altar in the name of the LORD: and he made a trench about the altar, as great as would contain two measures of seed.*
> [33] *And he put the wood in order, and cut the bullock in pieces, and laid him on the wood, and said, Fill four barrels with water, and pour it on the burnt sacrifice, and on the wood.*
> [34] *And he said, Do it the second time. And they did it the second time. And he said, Do it the third time. And they did it the third time.*
> [35] *And the water ran round about the altar; and he filled the trench also with water.*
> —1 Kings 18:31-35

Elijah wanted to prove beyond a shadow of a doubt that his God was sovereign, and Lord of all. He purposely doused his sacrifice with water over and over again, filling up even the trench that was around the altar.

36And it came to pass at the time of the offering of the evening sacrifice, that Elijah the prophet came near, and said, LORD God of Abraham, of Isaac, and of Israel, let it be known this day that thou art God in Israel, and that I am thy servant, and that I have done all these things at thy word. 37Hear me, O LORD, hear me, that this people may know that thou art the LORD God, and that thou hast turned their heart back again.

—1 Kings 18:36-37

Elijah places the emphasis on the Lord that God may be glorified and not himself, unlike the false prophets.

38Then the fire of the LORD fell, and consumed the burnt sacrifice, and the wood, and the stones, and the dust, and licked up the water that was in the trench.

—1 Kings 18:38

Elijah prayed that the people would know that Jehovah is God, and that their hearts would be turned toward God.This is an example of a powerful witnessing tool and prayer. Elijah is basically evangelizing, but not in the traditional "church message" method that many of us are used to. He is out in the field challenging 850 men and the king who all serve Baal. At any time they could have risen up against him and killed him, which was the norm for that day.

But Elijah was very confident. He was the one daring and challenging them. He knew that the supernatural abilities of God are endless, but he wanted the people of this kingdom to know that too. He wanted to introduce them to what he had been enjoying all along. This should be our burden and desire—to find a creative way to present Jesus to others; then pray that God would be honored by it; and that He would back us in what we say and do; and that He would turn the hearts of the people toward Him.

> [39]*And when all the people saw it, they fell on their faces: and they said, The LORD, he is the God; the LORD, he is the God.* [40]*And Elijah said unto them, Take the prophets of Baal; let not one of them escape. And they took them: and Elijah brought them down to the brook Kishon, and slew them there.*
> —1 Kings 18:39-40

Elijah's witnessing tool had worked. The people were convinced. They even confessed that this was **the** God. They fell on their faces in awe and in reverence of this Great and Mighty God. Then he slew all the false pro- phets, according to God's laws, for deceiving the kingdom.

Conclusion

Satan attempts to deceive the world by counterfeits. He has counterfeits for everything that God possesses. According to the Word, he uses signs and lying wonders. He has succeeded in convincing many, as proven in the story of Baal's prophets; but his power is limited and can never exceed God's.

God knows that Satan has the ability to even deceive the saints (Matthew 24:24), so He tells us in His Word:

> *Beloved, believe not every spirit, but try the spirits, whether they are of God: because many false prophets are gone out into the world.*
>
> —1 John 4:1

If we are unsure of something, God wants us to look it up in the Word of God to see if it is in His will for us. Even if we think we know something, we should take the time to check the Word to be sure that our thoughts are lining up with it. We don't ever want to glorify Satan by being tricked into doing his works. The Word says that we are not to be ignorant of Satan's devices (2 Corinthians 2:11). We are to be sober and vigilant, watching for the attacks of the enemy (1 Peter 5:8), so let's not be a people who are destroyed for a lack of knowledge (Hosea 4:6). Let us become equipped with the armor of God, and receive the mind of Christ, thereby proving God's sovereignty, and exposing Satan's subtle deception and limited power.

LESSON REVIEW

1. The sovereignty of God reveals Him as the supreme _____ and _____ over all the earth.

2. Name five characteristics of God's sovereignty and five of Satan's counter-feits.

3. Name the prophet who was bold enough to challenge 850 servants of Baal.
   How did he prove the sovereignty of God?

4. How is Satan able to deceive so many, according to the conclusion of this lesson?

Scripture References:

Psalms 103:19
2 Chronicles 6:14
Matthew 24:24
1 John 4:1
2 Corinthians 2:11
1 Peter 5:8
Hosea 4:6

The Day I Got Set Free

My Diary of Deliverance

The weapons of our warfare are not carnal, but mighty through God to the pulling down of strongholds. (1 Cor. 10:4)

Date: _____

- Monday
- Tuesday
- Wednesday
- Thursday
- Friday
- Saturday
- Sunday

**If two of you shall agree on earth as touching any thing that they shall ask, it shall be done for them.* (Matthew 18:19)*

Today Lord I set myself in agreement with Bishop George Bloomer and the mighty prayer warriors of Bethel Family Worship Center that this yoke will be destroyed in my life, in Jesus' name. Amen

_____

_____

_____

_____

_____

Personal Notes:

_____

_____

_____

_____

_____

_____

_____

_____

_____

_____

_____

_____

_____

_____

_____

_____

_____

_____

_____

LESSON 1: Satan, You're Not A Sovereign

_____

_____

_____

_____

_____

_____

_____

_____

_____

_____

_____

_____

_____

_____

_____

_____

_____

_____

_____

_____

_____

_____

_____

_____

_____

_____

_____

_____

_____

_____

_____

_____

_____

_____

_____

_____

_____

_____

LESSON

THE PLOT TO
DESTROY DESTINY

---

*The thief cometh not but to steal, and to
kill, and to destroy: I am come that they
might have life, and that they might have it
more abundantly.* —John 10:10

INTRODUCTION

From the beginning of time, until His death at Calvary's cross, Satan has sought to destroy the Savior and to rob the children of God of their destiny. In this lesson we will identify many of Satan's cunning tactics, and show how Jesus obtained victory over them all. We will discuss the stages of Jesus' life, and how Satan's plan was foiled throughout them.

Prayer

Lord Jesus,

I praise You for coming to earth to be our Savior, knowing all that You would have to endure. Your love is so great. May we truly gain a revelation of the enemy's tactics from your days on earth until now. Thank You for the power that You have given us over him. Amen.

LESSON

Destiny: inevitable necessity; divine decree; fate; that to which any person or thing is destined; fortune; doom.

Satan has been trying since the beginning of the world to destroy mankind. When Jesus came on the scene, Satan made every attempt possible, from Jesus' birth until even after His death, to annihilate Him and to prevent His influence among the people. Satan was the one who prompted Herod to destroy all the male children of Bethlehem ages two and under, in a foiled attempt to assassinate baby Jesus. He was also the one who tried to overcome Christ when Christ was weakened by fasting in the wilderness, and even suggested that Christ throw Himself down from the pinnacle of the Temple.

The attempt of the people to throw Christ from the hilltop at Nazareth, and the two storms on the sea of Galilee, were also plans of Satan to destroy Jesus Christ. When foiled in all of these attempts, Satan renewed the fight through priests, scribes, Pharisees, and Saduccees; but only seemed to succeed when he convinced Judas to sell His Master. Then, even amid the shades of Gethsemane, he sought to kill Christ by physical weakness before He could reach the cross to make atonement for all of our sins. This lesson explores Satan's tactics in trying to eradicate the Savior from the earth.

1. **Before Jesus' Birth**
2. **After His Birth**

3. Before Jesus' Ministry Began on Earth
4. During Jesus' Ministry
5. The Garden of Gethsemane
6. After His Death

BEFORE HIS BIRTH

It was the sole desire of Satan to prevent the manifestation of the coming of the Messiah to earth—the domain, which he now thought he ruled. He began with casting doubt into the mind of Joseph about the conception of the baby, which Mary carried. Was the child truly conceived of the heart of God through the power of the Holy Spirit? Should Joseph put his promised mate away in shame? Should he leave her ostracized and alone with her child – the One who would take away the sins of the world, though stigmatized with the label of a bastard? God would not allow the latter, so He convinced Joseph of the authenticity of His divinely orchestrated plan of conception for Mary's baby.

Satan's first battle plan had come to naught. For Joseph, fear and doubt gave way to a firm assurance of the plan of God, and he honored his marital agreement with Mary. Satan, however, did not become discouraged at this loss, and continued to wage war with our heavenly Father, His Son, and the plan of God to redeem His people.

Satan is found months later, as the fulfillment of time was drawing near, moving upon the mind of Caesar to declare a census for all the people—Satan's cunning way of finding the Savior and destroying Him immediately after His birth. Because of this declaration, Mary, the vessel that housed the promise, was then forced to make the long, hard trek to Bethlehem of Judea but the Father, in His loving providence, forbade their journey from bringing harm to the promise.

We must understand that whatever the plan of God is for our lives, no matter the assault of the enemy, God's divine providence will bring to pass His promise and destiny for our lives.

AFTER HIS BIRTH

In the latter part of 1 Peter 5:8, we are told that our *adversary, the devil, walks about as a roaring lion, seeking whom he may devour.* This was Satan's goal as he reached into his arsenal, once again, to find a weapon that would defeat the Sovereign God. King Herod was now the puppet being used in Satan's diabolic scheme to end the life of Christ (Read Matthew 2).

Wise men came to King Herod inquiring about where the King of the Jews had been born, that they might "worship" Him. Vexed with the thought of another king, Herod entreated the wise men to return to him upon locating this baby king, that he might also go and "pay homage to Him." God, being all-knowing, permitted an angel to instruct the wise men in a dream to continue on their journey home, for King Herod sought to do harm to the promise. They obeyed the instructions of God and did not return to the king.

The King, realizing that he would not retrieve the information he sought from the wise men, became infuriated and slaughtered all the male children, ages two and under, in the city of Bethlehem. But God foiled the stratagem of the enemy, warning Joseph also in a dream to flee with his family from harm's way into Egypt.

Satan, the father of lies and a deceiver, recognizes the excitement from the people regarding the new-coming King; so he "piggy-backs" off of this enthusiasm, proclaiming a lie through Herod—"bring me word again, that I may come and worship him also." Be wise to the devices of Satan. One of his many deceptions is to appear as an "angel of light," (2 Corinthians 11:14) only moments before lunging in for the kill.

BEFORE HIS MINISTRY BEGAN

Jesus grew to be a man. The call of the ministry was heavy upon Him as He was baptized by John the Baptist, and then led by the Spirit into the wilderness to be tempted of the devil who was all too ready to take on the challenge. So it was, as Christ was in the wilderness, having fasted forty days, the enemy made his move upon Jesus. Feeling that his foe was vulnerable, and weakened with hunger, Satan then enticed the Savior with the lust of the eye, the lust of the flesh, and the pride of life. He sought to play upon Jesus' hunger, and insisted that Jesus prove His position in the kingdom by turning stones into bread. Christ, having spent time in His Father's presence, however, drew the sword of the Spirit to contend with His enemy, saying, *It is written, man shall not live by bread alone, but by every word that proceedeth out of the mouth of God* (Matthew 4:4).

Satan, seeing Jesus to be a worthy opponent, hurls another temptation at Jesus by taking him to a high pinnacle, and encouraging Him to throw Himself down, using distorted scripture to convince Christ that this was a good idea, saying, *He shall give his angels charge concerning thee: and in their hands they shall bear thee up, lest at any time thou dash thy foot against a stone* (Matthew 4:6). Jesus struck back with the Word, and said to the enemy, *Thou shalt not tempt the Lord thy God* (Matthew 4:7). The enemy, unhappy, yet not convinced of his defeat, took Jesus upon a high mountain and showed Him all the kingdoms of the world, and their splendor. In his arrogance, the enemy said, *All these things will I give thee, if thou wilt fall down and worship me* (Matthew 4:9). Christ, tired of the enemy's games, let the devil know that He had not come to earth to entertain, nor did He have a need to prove His place in the Kingdom. He pierced Satan through the heart by saying, *Thou shalt worship the Lord thy God, and him only shalt thou serve* (Matthew 4:10). Finally, unable to stand under this last blow, Satan left the Savior in efforts to recuperate from the battle and to plan his next assault.

We realize that one of Satan's schemes is to attack when we are in our most vulnerable state. He waited until the Savior suffered from hunger to attack Him; but Christ had spent time before the Father and was able to defeat Satan with the Word, even in His weakened state.

DURING HIS MINISTRY

It was early morning. Christ had gotten out of bed, and proceeded to the temple, as He was accustomed to doing. When He sat down to teach the people as they gathered, Satan came to be a part, in the form of the scribes and the Pharisees. These people were an easy instrument for Satan to use because they were a self-righteous group of Jews living by the letter of the law, but they had no true fellowship with God. They were also a jealous group, and were insecure because they were losing control over the people, and of course the Pharisees would not have that. The scribes and the Pharisees conspired together to find aught with Jesus; so they brought before Him a woman found in adultery. Making clear to Him that this crime was punishable by death, according to the law, the scribes and Pharisees were desirous to see how Jesus would resolve this matter. Christ responded by stooping, and writing something on the ground. He was very slow to speak. The scribes and the Pharisees continued to ask Him for an answer. Jesus stood and looked at them and said, *He that is without sin among you, let him first cast a stone at her* (John 8:7). All that heard, fell under conviction and left the temple. Jesus then excused her without condemnation, and told her to sin no more. The Pharisees again approached Him after this incident, complaining that He bore witness of Himself. Pharisees felt that man could swear by no one but God, but Jesus let them know that He can swear by Himself, and that the Father would honor it. The Pharisees grew angry, but God had tied the hand of Satan, preventing him from doing harm to Christ because it was not yet His time.

In the preceding passage, Satan sought to discredit the ministry and message of Jesus as he continues to do within the ministry of Jesus' modern-day disciples—the saints of God. Jesus, nonetheless, in His infinite wisdom, does not fall prey to Satan's trap of condemning the woman, but instead exhibits to the crowd His ministry of compassion, as He restores her to the fellowship, instead of casting her away.

Many ministries today are destroyed because the crowd demands blood from individuals who've strayed. And in an effort to please the crowd, leaders, oftentimes, negligently throw the carcasses of the injured to predators who devour them, as they wait patiently for the next unsuspecting victim. As the crowd is fed, many injured lives are needlessly lost.

THE GARDEN OF GETHSEMANE

In the garden, Christ had come to pray many times, but on this night, His heart was heavy as His time here on earth was drawing to a close. In Mark 14:35, Christ is seen asking the Father if it were possible to let the cup pass from Him. Christ was sorrowful, not because He would give up His life for the world, but because of the thought of being separated from His Father. Christ and His Father had never been separated by anything. Satan and his cohorts were there in the garden to buffet Christ. I am sure that they were taunting Him and telling Him that His upcoming death on the cross would not be a great enough sacrifice to atone for sin; and that He would eternally be separated from His Father. There was a real war going on in the garden. The gospel of Luke describes the sweat that fell from His countenance like as great drops of blood; but Christ thinks back on the integrity and faithfulness of His Father, and He says, *Nevertheless, thy will be done.*

AFTER HIS DEATH

In all of his strategic planning to still the life, the voice, and the purpose of Christ, Satan did not prevail. In a last ditch effort, he thought that he could hold the body of Christ by placing a stone over the mouth of the tomb, and also by securing the tomb with two armed guards and his demonic hosts. Satan was well aware that once the Savior arose, He would rise with all power, and with the keys to death, hell, and the grave. This same power would later be passed on to the saints as weapons for Satan's sure and timely demise. For the Bible declares that greater works shall we do.

In Luke 10:19, Jesus assures His disciples of their authority in Him over the enemy (Satan and his camp):

Behold, I give unto you power to tread on serpents and scorpions and over all the power of the enemy: and nothing shall by any means hurt you.
—Luke 10:19

Conclusion

Satan has always tried to destroy mankind, but has always been unsuccessful. When the Son of God came to earth, Satan tried to have Him killed. Before Jesus' birth, before He actually began ministering, during His ministry, and even after His death, Satan always attempted to get rid of Him. Satan's attempts have always been foiled, for Jesus made a show of Satan and all of the underworld openly. God has given us power – the capacity or ability to be effective against our foe – and He has given us the authority to tread – press beneath the foot of, or trample Satan, his demons, and all the power of the enemy. It is up to us to arm ourselves with the knowledge of God's Word, and be able to employ our weapons skillfully. Jesus is Lord, Satan is defeated, and nothing that Satan tries to do shall prevail unless we allow it. He is overcome by the blood of the Lamb and by the word of our testimony (Revelation 12:11).

****

LESSON REVIEW

1. How did Satan work in the mind of Joseph, Jesus' earthly father?

2. Caesar declared a census after the birth of Jesus. Name an Old Testament king who was also moved by Satan to declare a census.

3. In Matthew chapter two, King Herod, in an attempt to assassinate baby Jesus, ordered all baby boys, ages two and under, to be killed. A similar situation took place in the Old Testament.

   a) Name the Old Testament king who ordered the assassination.
   b) Name the baby who was to be killed.
   c) Give the scripture reference.

4. How did Jesus defeat the enemy while He was in the wilderness?

5. What groups did Satan use to attack Jesus?

6. Christ has defeated the enemy, and now holds the keys to what? Where can this scripture be found?

Scripture References:

John 10:10
1 Peter 5:8
Matthew 2
2 Corinthians 11:14
Matthew 4:4,6,7,9-10
John 8:7
Mark 14:35
Luke 10:19
Revelation 12:11

The Day I Got Set Free

My Diary of Deliverance

The weapons of our warfare are not carnal, but mighty through God to the pulling down of strongholds. (1 Cor. 10:4)

Date: _____

- ☐ Monday
- ☐ Tuesday
- ☐ Wednesday
- ☐ Thursday
- ☐ Friday
- ☐ Saturday
- ☐ Sunday

**If two of you shall agree on earth as touching any thing that they shall ask, it shall be done for them. (Matthew 18:19)

Today Lord I set myself in agreement with Bishop George Bloomer and the mighty prayer warriors of Bethel Family Worship Center that this yoke will be destroyed in my life, in Jesus' name. Amen

_____

_____

_____

_____

_____

_____

_____

_____

_____

_____

_____

_____

_____

_____

_____

_____

_____

_____

_____

_____

_____

_____

_____

_____

LESSON 2: The Plot to Destroy Destiny

WEAPONS FOR WARRIORS

_____

_____

_____

_____

_____

_____

_____

_____

_____

_____

_____

_____

_____

_____

_____

_____

_____

_____

LESSON

SATAN'S FALL AND HOLY WAR

Pride goeth before destruction, and an haughty spirit before a fall.
—Proverbs 16:18

INTRODUCTION
LUCIFER'S ORIGIN

The origin and history of Lucifer is revealed in Ezekiel 28:12-19, and also in Isaiah 14:11-17. You will find that Lucifer was *an anointed cherub* (Ezekiel 28:14)—the *son of the morning* (Isaiah 14:12). He was *perfect in his ways* (Ezekiel 28:12) and full of wisdom (Ezekiel 28:12). He was filled with music (Ezekiel 28:13), and perfect in beauty (Ezekiel 28:15). He walked on stones of fire, and had complete access to the holy mountain of God (Ezekiel 28:14). Why would someone with all of these privileges just throw them all away? What happened to make him lose this prestigious position in heaven and become such a horrid being?

Well, Isaiah 14:11-17 explains that Satan wanted to make himself like God (verse 14). He wanted to exalt his throne above God's (verse 13). He simply became proud. The Word says that there is none below, beside, or above God (Deuteronomy 4:39; 1 Kings 8:22). So Satan was cast down to earth as a direct result of his sin.

Prayer

Lord Jesus,

I am gaining insight into the character of Satan and his fall. Why would he even give up a privilege so great? He is mad at me because I now intend to live where he can never re-enter, and that is with You. Thank you for bestowing so great a privilege on such a sinner as I. Amen.

LESSON

As the eyes of God perused Paradise, there loomed a foul stench, never before smelled in the heavens. The All-Knowing One knew that the fruit of iniqulty had found its way into the Kingdom of Light. He knew exactly where, and from whom, this fruit had originated: LUCIFER. "Lucifer: the quintessence (model) of perfection, endowed with great wisdom and exquisite in your beauty. You were meticulously fashioned with every precious stone, the sardius, topaz and the diamond to name a few. Your very settings and mountings were created with gold, especially with you in mind. You were the anointed cherub, chosen to guard the Holy Mountain of God (Ezekiel 28:12-14). Many writers say that you were like the rays seen before sunrise, ushering in the presence of God." How could one who enjoyed the presence and abundance of a loving God, now give off the odor that was polluting Heaven?

> *How art thou fallen from heaven, O Lucifer, son of the morning! How art thou cut down to the ground, which didst weaken the nations?*
> *For thou hast said in thine heart, I **will** ascend into the heaven, I **will** exalt my throne above the stars of God; I **will** sit also upon the mount of the congregation, in the sides of the north; I **will** ascend above the heights of the clouds; I **will** be like the Most High.*
> —Isaiah 14:12-14

The prophet Isaiah, in the above scripture, presents Lucifer's five statements that incriminated him and caused his expulsion from heaven.

The Five "I Wills"

1. I will ascend into heaven.
2. I will exalt my throne above the stars of God.
3. I will sit also upon the mountain of the congregation, in the sides of the North.
4. I will ascend above the heights of the clouds.

5. I will be like the Most High.

1. I WILL ASCEND INTO HEAVEN.

Having a great rank in heaven was not enough for Lucifer. He had peered, as some would put it, too intently on the other side of the fence. He had witnessed God's Almighty power, Sovereign judgment and Majestic beauty; and the grass was looking greener on the other side. Lucifer had begun to lustfully covet the person of God. To pattern himself after God was not enough for him. His inordinate desire led to emulation, and we find him in Isaiah declaring to rise to divine authority in an already occupied territory, The Heavens. How can one take possession of something that is already occupied? He must oust the current occupant.

2. I WILL EXALT MY THRONE ABOVE THE STARS OF GOD.

God had already given Lucifer great authority, for the Word speaks of him having a throne, but Lucifer envisioned himself establishing his dominion over all the other angels – created beings like himself. The term "star" has often referred to angelic beings in scripture. Lucifer's name itself means "day star," or "star of the morning." Lucifer is depicted in Revelations 12:3&4 as a great, red dragon whose tail drew the third part of the stars from heaven and cast them to the earth. The book of Job 38:7 also makes reference to the stars, although unclear. God is questioning Job, "Where were you when the morning stars sang together and all the sons of God shouted for joy?"

3. **I WILL SIT ALSO UPON THE MOUNT OF CONGREGATION, IN THE SIDES OF THE NORTH.** Lucifer does not stop his delusions of grandeur, but proceeds to reserve himself a seat at the summit of the heavenly mountain; at the point around which the heavenly bodies turned and the throne of God resided.

4. **I WILL ASCEND ABOVE THE HEIGHTS OF THE CLOUDS.** Lucifer seeks to rise above and surpass all to be second to none.

5. **I WILL BE LIKE THE MOST HIGH.** In Lucifer's drunken thirst for power, he loses himself and proclaims he will be like the El' Elyon, the Most High God. In other words, he will have sovereign rule and will be equal to Almighty God.

INGREDIENTS FOR A FALL AND EXPULSION FROM YOUR DIVINELY APPOINTED POSITION:

1. **Covetousness** - excessive or culpable desire of the possession of another
2. **Jealousy** - resentment or bitterness in rivalry; envy.
3. **Pride** - an excessive high opinion of oneself. Arrogant or disdainful conduct or treatment.
4. **Rebellion** - to act or a show of defiance toward an authority or a convention.

Covetousness + Jealousy + Pride + Rebellion = Expulsion from divine appointment

In the "Five I wills," Lucifer exhibits all of the above traits. We must be very careful when admiring the anointing and abilities of another, that we do not begin to covet, or become jealous, prideful, or rebellious. God felt so strongly about this that He included instructions in the Ten Commandments.

> *Thou shall not covet thy neighbor's house, thy neighbor's wife, nor his servant, nor his maidservant, nor his ox, nor his ass, or anything that is thy neighbor's.*
> —Exodus 20:1

HOW DOES GOD RESPOND TO THIS OPEN REBELLION AND DECLARATION OF WAR?

*⁷Then war broke out in heaven; Michael and his angels fought.
⁸But they were defeated, and there was no room found for them in heaven any longer.
⁹And the huge dragon was cast down and out - that age-old serpent, who is called the Devil and Satan, he who is the seducer (deceiver) of all humanity the world over; he was forced out and down to the earth, and his angels were flung out along with him.*
—Revelation 12:7-9

SATAN'S REACTION TO EVICTION

¹³And when the dragon saw that he was cast unto the earth, he persecuted the woman which brought forth the man child.

¹⁷And the dragon was wroth with the woman, and went away to make war with the remnant of her seed, which keep the commandments of God, and have the testimony of Jesus Christ:
—Revelation 12:13,17

¹Now the serpent was more subtil than any beast of the field which the LORD God had made. And he said unto the

woman, Yea, hath God said, Ye shall not eat of every tree of the garden?

[4]And the serpent said unto the woman, Ye shall not surely die.
[5]For God doth know that in the day ye eat thereof, then your eyes shall be opened, and ye shall be as gods, knowing good and evil.
—Genesis 3:1,4-5

Satan is much like a jealous woman who once experienced the pleasure of a good man. He is angry at God's new love (the saints), and is doing all he can to destroy and come between that relationship. The thought of God's creation enjoying any part of what he once had angers him. And just like a jealous woman, he seeks to get back at the One who will no longer put up with his foolishness by trying to hurt the object of God's affections (the saints).

SATAN'S FATE

1. Before the end

[2]And he laid hold on the dragon, that old serpent, which is the Devil and Satan, and bound him a thousand years,
[3]And cast him into the bottomless pit, and shut him up, and set a seal upon

him, that he should deceive the nations no more, till the thousand years should be fulfilled: and after that he must be loosed a little season.

—Revelation 20:2-3

2. After his release

[7]And when the thousand years are expired, Satan shall be loosed out of his prison,
[8]And shall go out to deceive the nations which are in the four quarters of the earth, Gog and Magog, to gather them together to battle: the number of whom is as the sand of the sea.

—Revelation 20:7-8

3. The Final Face-Off

[17]Thine heart was lifted up because of thy beauty, thou hast corrupted thy wisdom by reason of thy brightness: I will cast thee to the ground, I will lay thee before kings, that they may behold thee.
[18] Thou hast defiled thy sanctuaries by the multitude of thine iniquities by the multitude of thy iniquities, by the iniquity of thy traffick; therefore will I bring forth a fire from the midst of thee; it shall devour thee, and I will bring

thee to ashes upon the earth in the sight of all them that behold thee.

—Ezekiel 28:17-18

[1]For, behold, the day cometh, that shall burn as an oven; and all the proud, yea, and all that do wickedly, shall be stubble: and the day that cometh shall burn them up, saith the LORD of hosts, that it shall leave them neither root nor branch.

[3]And ye shall tread down the wicked; for they shall be ashes under the soles of your feet in the day that I shall do this, saith the LORD of hosts.

—Malachi 4:1,3

[7]And when the thousand years are expired, Satan shall be loosed out of his prison,
[8]and shall go out to deceive the nations which are in the four quarters of the earth, Gog and Magog, to gather them together to battle: the number of whom is as the sand of the sea.
[9]And they went up on the breadth of the earth, and compassed the camp of the saints about, and the beloved city: and fire came down from God out of heaven, and devoured them.
[10]And the devil that deceived them was cast into the lake of fire and brimstone,

*where are also the beast and the false
prophet are, and shall be tormented
day and night for ever and ever.*
—Revelation 20:7-8

Conclusion

Satan is a defeated foe. The battle has been
fought, the war won. Our job is to hold fast our
profession of faith (Hebrews 10:23-25), put on
the whole armor (Ephesians 6:10-18) and hide
the Word of God in our hearts (Psalms
119:11).

*Ye are of God, little children, and have
overcome them: because greater is he
that is in you, than he that is in the
world.*
—1 John 4:4

*Nay, in all these things we are more
than conquerors through him that loved
us.*
—Romans 8:37

*And they overcame him by the blood of
the Lamb, and by the word of their
testimony; and they loved not their
lives unto death.*
—Revelation 12:11

****

LESSON REVIEW

1. Name the "Five I Wills." In what scripture text are they found?

2. Name three jewels that once adorned Lucifer in heaven.

3. Name the ingredients for expulsion from divine appointment.

4. Who is Satan jealous of and why?

5. What position did Lucifer desire to overtake in heaven?

6. List two of Lucifer's titles before his fall.

Scripture References:

Proverbs 16:18
Ezekiel 28:12-19
Isaiah 14:11-17
Deuteronomy 4:39
Genesis 3:1,4-5
1 Kings 8:22
Revelation 12:3-4, 7-9, 13,17; 20:2-3
Job 38:7

The Day I Got Set Free

My Diary of Deliverance

The weapons of our warfare are not carnal, but mighty through God to the pulling down of strongholds. (1 Cor. 10:4)

Date: _____

- ❑ Monday
- ❑ Tuesday
- ❑ Wednesday
- ❑ Thursday
- ❑ Friday
- ❑ Saturday
- ❑ Sunday

***If two of you shall agree on earth as touching any thing that they shall ask, it shall be done for them. (Matthew 18:19)*

Today Lord I set myself in agreement with Bishop George Bloomer and the mighty prayer warriors of Bethel Family Worship Center that this yoke will be destroyed in my life, in Jesus' name. Amen

_____

_____

_____

_____

_____

LESSON 3: Satan's Fall and Holy War

_____

_____

_____

_____

_____

_____

_____

_____

_____

_____

_____

_____

_____

_____

_____

_____

_____

_____

_____

_____

_____

_____

_____

_____

_____

_____

_____

_____

_____

_____

_____

_____

_____

_____

_____

_____

_____

_____

_____

LESSON 3: Satan's Fall and Holy War

_____

_____

_____

_____

_____

_____

_____

_____

_____

_____

_____

_____

_____

_____

_____

_____

_____

_____

_____

_____

_____

LESSON

KNOWING YOUR ADVERSARY

*Finally, my brethren, be strong in the
Lord, and in the power of his might.*
                    —Ephesians 6:10-12

INTRODUCTION

Satan's continual effort, as stated in John 10:10, is *to steal, to kill, and to destroy.* However, Satan is not omnipresent; so how is he able to cause so much havoc throughout the world? Is he able to create all of this chaos by himself, or does he have assistance? If he has workers, where did they come from, and what are their names? This lesson will answer all of these questions and more. It will reveal the make-up of the underworld, its functions, and our God-given authority over it.

1. **Demons** - disembodied spirits who take possession of human bodies
2. **Principalities** - ruling authorities; princes in their palaces; territorial spirits
3. **Princes** - territorial powers who control certain nations, states, etc.
4. **Familiar spirits** - spirits that impersonate the dead
5. **Wandering spirits** - spirits who do not possess a body but exercise outward control through hypnosis and oppression, for example, thus weakening their victims. They also direct mediums on what to say during seances.

Prayer

Lord Jesus,

Just like Elijah's apprentice, Elisha, You have opened our eyes to the beings present in the heavenlies and we thank You for enlightening our understanding. Give us wisdom, and give us strength as we yield ourselves to You, thus waging war on the enemy. Amen.

LESSON

WHERE SATAN'S ASSISTANTS CAME FROM

Demons: disembodied spirits

> *...Satan, which deceiveth the whole world: he was cast out into the earth, and his angels were cast out with him.*
>
> —Revelation 12:9

> *...Depart from me, ye cursed, into everlasting fire, prepared for the devil and his angels...*
>
> —Matthew 25:41

It is evident that Satan does have workers to assist him in his seemingly endless feats. They are fallen angels who joined with Satan in rebellion against God and were consequently cast down. Their original habitation was in heaven (Revelation 12:8) as angels of the Lord but Jude 6 says that they *kept not their first estate, but left their own habitation.* They sinned and were cast down, so now they temporarily inhabit the heavenlies (Ephesians 3:10)—the unseen spiritual realm. Scholars believe that one-third of them were thrown out of heaven because Revelation 12:4 states: *And his tail drew the third part of the stars of heaven, and did cast them to the earth...*

THEIR NAMES

There are several names listed in scripture in reference to Satan's aides:

1. *demons* (James 2:19; Luke 10:17)
2. *authorities* (Ephesians 1:21)
3. *princes* (Daniel 10:13; Ezekiel 28:13)
4. *thrones* (Colossians 1:16)
5. *powers* (Ephesians 1:21, 3:10; Colossians 1:16)
6. *familiar spirits* (Leviticus 20:27; Isaiah 8:19)
7. *seducing spirits* (1 Timothy 4:1)
8. *devils* (1 Timothy 4:1)
9. *unclean spirits* (Matthew 10:1; Mark 6:7)

10. *evil spirits* (Luke 7:21; Acts 19: 12,13)
11. *spirits in prison* (1 Peter 3:18-20)
12. *wandering spirits* (Jude 13)

HIERARCHY

It is strongly suggested within Christendom that there is a hierarchical structure, or at least several departments within Satan's kingdom. It would seem rather obvious, in my opinion, that there is a hierarchy since Satan was the *son of the morning* (Isaiah 14:12) — the chief of the angels in heaven — that he would have formed a comparable structure in his domain as well. However, it is definitely evident that they have all been designated in various ways.

ABILITIES IN THE HEAVENLIES

In the book of Daniel (Daniel 10:12-14), an angel of the Lord explains to Daniel that his prayer to God was heard the minute that he prayed, but a demon hindered the angel's ability to deliver the answer immediately.

This story does not suggest that Satan or his forces have more power than that of our Heavenly Father. Absolutely not! It is recorded in Revelation 12 that there was war in heaven and Michael and his angels fought against

Satan and his angels (verse 7) but Satan and his angels did not prevail (verse 8). Then in Revelation 20:1-3, it is clearly seen that God's angels are more powerful than demons. That is because the angels of the Lord operate out of God's power. An angel is depicted holding the key to the bottomless pit, along with a heavy chain (verse 1). He laid hold of Satan, bound Satan with the chain, and cast Satan into the bottomless pit for 1,000 years (verses 2-3).

In the story of the Daniel's hindered prayer (Daniel 10:12-14), the Word is only making it apparent that there is a reality that extends beyond our perceptions. Angels, both good and evil, are presented in this text as real beings who are actively at work in our lives. The angels of the Lord carry out divine commands, while the powers of darkness hinder, corrupt, confuse and destroy. Though these demonic powers afflict us and cause us trouble, we can rest in the knowledge that Jesus Christ has already defeated them, and that their end is soon to come.

Satan's power is limited, and cannot compare to God's. If you read Job 1:6-12, you will discover that Satan can only do what God allows. God allows Satan to work in our lives, not because He is uncaring, but because He desires for us to become built up in our most holy faith. Satan is already a defeated foe. The Word has already described his end in

Revelation 20:10—he will be *cast into the lake of fire and brimstone...and shall be tormented day and night forever and ever.*

LEGAL AUTHORITY ON EARTH

Revelation 13:7 says:

And it was given unto him to make war with the saints, and to overcome them: and power was given him over all kindreds, and tongues, and nations.

There are certain functions that come along with Satan's job. A few of his job descriptions are listed as the following:

1. *a thief* (John 10:10)
2. *one who comes to steal, kill, and destroy* (John 10:10)
3. *the father of lies* (John 8:44)
4. *a murderer* (John 8:44)
5. *one who seeks to devour* (1 Peter 5:8)
6. *a deceiver* (Revelation 12:9, 13:14, 20:7,8)
7. *a performer of great signs* (Revelation 13:13)
8. *accuser of the brethren* (Revelation 12:10)
9. *the lawless one...with all power, lying wonders, signs, and unright-*

eous deceptions (2 Thessalonians 2:8 - NKJV)

10. *son of perdition...sits as God in the temple of God* (2 Thessalonians 2:3,4)
11. *god of this world...blinding the minds of people* (2 Corinthians 4:4)
12. *prince of this world* (John 14:30)
13. *one who can transform himself into an angel of light* (2 Corinthians 11:14)
14. *prince of the powers of the air* (Ephesians 2:2)
15. *adversary* (1 Peter 5:8)
16. *serpent* (Revelation 12:9)
17. *enemy* (Matthew 13:28)

His workers are called "ministers" who are able to transform themselves into ministers of righteousness (2 Corinthians 11:15). They perform signs (Revelation 16:14) and create doctrines (1 Timothy 4:1). They are also deceivers (1 Timothy 4:1).

DO WE HAVE POWER OVER THESE DARK FORCES?

At this point, you may be wondering if humans have the ability to fight against demons. Certainly, but not in the way that you may think. Ephesians 6:12 explains that we are not fighting a physical war, but a spiritual one, which can only be combated with spiritual weaponry. Verses 13 through 17 of the same chapter describe these weapons as the armor of God, which are comprised of:

1. the helmet of salvation
2. the breastplate of righteousness
3. truth, with which we gird our loins
4. the preparation of the gospel of peace, with which we shod our feet
5. the shield of faith
6. the sword of the Spirit (the Word of God)

Ephesians 6:18 then admonishes us to also use the weapon of prayer—praying always, and praying in the Spirit, while being watchful for oneself and the saints.

Conclusion

Satan is the employer of a host of fallen angels. They were cast down with him, because of their rebellion. They are known by several names, but are most often called fallen angels or demons. They carry out Satan's orders, whose ultimate goal is to steal, kill, and destroy (John 10:10). However, we have authority over the enemy (his entire kingdom included), and we can fight against him through prayer, faith, truth, the Word, righteousness, salvation, and the preparation of the gospel of peace. The Word says that he is a defeated foe (Hebrews 2:14; Colossians 2:15); therefore we have no need to fear him. *Greater is he that is in* you, *than he that is in the world* (1 John 4:4).

****

LESSON REVIEW

1. Name five types of powers of darkness.

2. What is the significance of Daniel's prayer being hindered in Daniel 10:12-14?

3. What are Satan's three major duties, and what scripture text is it taken from?

4. Name four of Satan's job descriptions.

5. Name the seven pieces of the armor of God and their functions.

Scripture References:

Ephesians 6:10-12; 3:10;1:21; 2:2
John 10:10; 8:44; 14:30
Revelation 12:4,7-10; 20:1-3,7-8, 10; 13:7,13-14; 16:14
Matthew 25:41;10:1; 13:28
Jude 6,13
Luke 10:17;7:21
Daniel 10:12-14
Ezekiel 28:13
Colossians 1:16
Leviticus 20:27
Isaiah 8:19; 14:12

The Day I Got Set Free

My Diary of Deliverance

The weapons of our warfare are not carnal, but mighty through God to the pulling down of strongholds. (1 Cor. 10:4)

Date: _____

- ❏ Monday
- ❏ Tuesday
- ❏ Wednesday
- ❏ Thursday
- ❏ Friday
- ❏ Saturday
- ❏ Sunday

**If two of you shall agree on earth as touching any thing that they shall ask, it shall be done for them. (Matthew 18:19)

Today Lord I set myself in agreement with Bishop George Bloomer and the mighty prayer warriors of Bethel Family Worship Center that this yoke will be destroyed in my life, in Jesus' name. Amen

_____

_____

_____

_____

_____

LESSON 4: Knowing Your Adversary

_____

_____

_____

_____

_____

_____

_____

_____

_____

_____

_____

_____

_____

_____

_____

_____

_____

_____

LESSON 4: Knowing Your Adversary

_____

_____

_____

_____

_____

_____

_____

_____

_____

_____

_____

_____

_____

_____

_____

_____

_____

_____

_____

_____

_____

_____

_____

LESSON

DEMONOLOGYAND GOVERNMENTS

For we wrestle not against flesh and blood, but against principalities, against powers, against the rulers of the darkness of this world, against spiritual wickedness in high places. —Ephesians 6:12

INTRODUCTION

As Christians we are continually reminded that the struggle between good and evil is ever present. We live in a fallen world that is unfavorable to the Gospel. The structural powers in our government are tainted with greed, pride, and deceit. There is a constant satanic pressure and attack on the family that is, in some ways, generated from the government. Today's Church irresponsibly sits back with their arms folded watching the government reach out by providing food, shelter and clothing to the unfortunate. Jesus left on record in Matthew 25:34-45 that as ambassadors of Christ, we are responsible for feeding the hungry, clothing the naked, taking in the stranger, and so on. But because we have lost our first love, we have loosened the seams of our authority and purpose in the world, and strengthened the governments' borders with control.

Consequently, the strong man in the government seemingly cannot be overcome unless we, who are spiritually discerned, begin using the teachings of Christ on "loosing" and "binding." We must first bind the strong man that Satan has placed in the governmental systems, that the will of God may be loosed in the land. Then, we who love the Lord, should practice what we preach and do the will of Him Who sent us. We know that the weapons of

our warfare are not carnal but mighty (2
Corinthians 10:4), therefore we need to fight
the good fight of faith against the forces of
Satan. In Jesus Name!

Prayer

Lord Jesus,

Though Satan seeks to defeat us in living a
Christian life in every way possible, we still
have victory through Your Lordship, and we
thank You. We thank You that although he is
the god of this world, including its governments, we are not of this world. We confess
that the weapons of our warfare are not carnal,
but mighty through You to the pulling down of
the strongholds (2 Corinthians 10:4) that the
enemy has set up across this nation. He
desires to hold back Your plan, O Lord, but we
know that You have made a show of him
openly once, and will do it again. We know
that Your Word says that every knee shall bow
and every tongue shall confess You as Lord.
Everyone, including the government, has to
submit to You. So we pray that You would
touch the hearts of those within the government system to move according to Your will.
We also know that nothing can happen without
Your permission, so we thank You that all
events, good or bad, are to glorify You. In
Jesus' name. Amen.

LESSON

Demonology – the study or belief in demons or demonism

Satan – the devil, Lucifer (morning star), prince of darkness, chief of the devils, great adversary of man, father of lies, deceiver, accuser of the brethren, tempter, thief, the god of this world, prince of the power of the air

Demon – disembodied spirit

Government – the act of governing, regime, direction, system of administration by which a community, country, state, nation is managed, administering the laws, authority of one officially in control.

Legate (Delegate) – appointed to act for another or others, sent as a representative or ambassador with authority and power to act, a district governed by a legate, has the right to participate in debates

IN EARTH AS IT IS IN HEAVEN

Authority – the right to command and enforce obedience, the right to act officially, authorize, endowed with authority, formally sanctioned, justify, commission, accepted as authoritative

Compromise – an adjustment for settlement by arbitration and mutual concession, usually involving a partial surrender of purposes or principles.

Will – the power of conscious, deliberate action by which the rational mind makes choice of its ends of action and directs the energies in carrying out its strong determinations, a concious inclination toward any end or course.

There is an order that is set in the earth as well as in the heavens. God created man in his own image and gave man something that no other creature possesses and that is a will. A *will* is the power to make choices and carry out its determinations. God gave Adam dominion over all the living creatures and instructed him to replenish the earth and subdue it. (Gen.1:28). From the rib of man God created Eve and instructed her and Adam to be fruitful and multiply. Adam's job was caretaker of the Garden of Eden and Eve's role was to be a help meet.

Under this dominion mandate, mankind...

(1) was given spiritual authority over the created world to represent the source of power in the world, that is God

(2) had to exercise authority of that power over creation to make sure that God's

will was done in earth as it is in heaven and

(3) had to be good stewards, being accountable daily to God for the way in which they fulfilled their role.

Adam and Eve's life in the garden was complete. They had everything they needed. In other words they literally had heaven on earth. However, there was one stipulation to this heavenly bliss and that was to eat of all the trees in the garden except for one, the Tree of Good and Evil. We all know the story. The serpent beguiled Eve to eat the forbidden fruit from that tree and Eve in turn coaxed Adam to eat. Although Adam knew the voice of God, he willfully compromised God's Word. This act of disobedience to God's word opened the door to sin in the earth and closed the door of redemption in heaven.

From the foundations of the world until now, these rights were never intended for Satan's use, but obedience to sin caused the fall of mankind. Sin has ruined not only mankind, but also all of creation (Romans 8:22). Man lost access to the presence of God, and his authority over the world collapsed. Now Satan has authority to be ruler of this world, and prince of the powers of the air. The problems of society are not merely due to the sinfulness of fallen men, but there is also structural evil—evil in the world systems. All the structures of society, the principalities and powers, are also sin-damaged. But if sin has penetrated the fabric of society, so has the Blood of Jesus (Rom. 5:20). For the Blood reaches as far as sin has spread.

UNRIGHTEOUS LEADERSHIP

1. Why were so many of Israel's kings wicked?

Many of their hearts were hardened against the True and Living God, thus they entered into idolatry and served false gods. We know that the steps of a good man are ordered by the Lord (Ps 37:23) but from King Rehoboam to King Zedekiah, the majority of Israel's kings had a wicked heart and did evil in the sight of the Lord.

2. What ordered their footsteps in the way of Baal instead of in the way of God?

Compromise! The influences of Satan are targeted at those in authority who have the ability to make major changes in the standards, morals and fundamentals of an establishment. This attack, from the forces of Satan, is disguised behind the word "compromise".

"Compromise" is defined as *an adjustment or a surrender of intended purposes or principles.*

Anytime compromise is exercised, the original intent or purpose is challenged and thus changed. Compromise is appropriate in many given situations except when it involves altering the infallible Word of God.

Righteousness exalteth a nation: but sin is a reproach to any people (Pr 14:34). Whenever leaders exercise control without acknowledging God, Who gives control, they are practicing a form of witchcraft. Witchcraft is the attempt to bend the will of someone to make it agree with the person practicing witchcraft. It is also the refusal to acknowledge God as being in control. When will we learn from our examples that *rebellion to God's Word is as the sin of witchcraft and stubbornness is as iniquity and idolatry?*

In the book of Samuel, Israel was granted their first king, whose name was Saul. Saul was commanded by the Lord to wipe out their enemy, the Amalekites, but instead he compromised with the voice of the people and made his own commandment, which was contrary to the Word of God. This act caused him to lose favor with God and also lose his reign as Israel's king. Because of his disobedience and pride, God withdrew His spirit from Saul and vexed him with an evil spirit from the Lord (1Sam 15).

In Daniel chapter four, we see where pride comes before a fall in the life of the king of Babylon, Nebuchadnezzar. He was full of pride and began to boast about all that his mighty hand had accomplished. In other words, the forces of Satan had blinded him to the point that he thought he was the preeminent force behind all Babylon's victories. Nevertheless, he soon found out that there is none other God like the Father of Abraham, Isaac and Jacob. Nebuchadnezzar learned the hard way that God gives kingdoms to whom He will, and He doeth what He will in the army of heaven, and with the inhabitants of the earth, for He is the King of heaven. Nebuchadnezzar lost his mind and became as a wild beast of the field because of his pride (Dan 4:25, 35, 37). But when he acknowledged Who reigned in the heavens, he gave glory to God and was restored to his position as king.

PRIDE BREEDS IGNORANCE AND HATE

From ancient history until now we have read about countless murders by ruthless rulers in government and today we read and see it in our daily newspaper, television, radio, etc. In the early 1900s, Adolph Hitler, tyrant of Germany lead a group called the Nazis. This organization origin was of a Christian nature but became corrupt. The Nazi symbol is a distorted cross. It is a hate group toward Jews,

Blacks, and gypsies. During Hitler's reign the slaughter of 6 million Jews was committed. In the scriptures we read of many unrighteous acts committed by pharaohs, kings, governors, herods and princes. The slaughter of innocent Hebrew babies by the Pharaoh of Egypt (Exodus 1:22) and the slaughter of babies age two and younger by King Herod (Matt 2:16), were both operations of the forces of Satan to stop God's redemptive plan, Moses the deliverer of Israel and Jesus the Savior of the world. Likewise, today's leaders are also being influenced by spiritual wickedness in high places. According to an article in The Wall Street Journal one of our U.S. Presidents, Ronald Reagan, during his reign, took the advice of a witch whom his wife Nancy had sought answers regarding a governmental issue as did King Saul when he consulted the witch of Endor found in 1Samuel 28:7.

Many renown leaders in our churches today have been blinded by the powers of Satan. The Million Man March is a prime example that our leaders are not spiritually discerned in the things of God. Many of our African-American leaders compromised their belief in righeous-ness and were not opposed to the march, the message, or the messenger. How can this be? The leader of this march was an antichrist of the '90s. This so-called Honorable Minister of the Black Muslim sect in the United States, proclaimed that God had inspired him to call

LESSON 5: Demonology and Governments

this march on Washington D.C. His religious beliefs, anti-Semitic attitude, and views of racial separation not discerned by the Christian community as a deception from the enemy. This kind of behavior from our Christian leaders is inexcusable. The church is in a regressive state because the blind is leading the blind and they shall all fall into a pit.

In the book of Revelation, chapter two, warnings are given to the angel (pastor) of the seven churches of Asia Minor. The church at Thyatira included every kind of worldliness and demon-inspired corruption of the truth (1 Tim 4:1-4). These doctrines were called "the deep things of God" by their advocates, but the Lord styles them as "the deep things of Satan". In the church of Smyrna the term "the synagogue of Satan" is mentioned. This congregation consisted of Jews who persecuted the Christians, because of their misguided zeal for the law of Moses, who, professing to worship God, really served Satan. Many of their problems, shortcomings and failures is prevalent in our church today. However, there is a redemptive plan for us...if he that hath an ear, would hear what the Spirit saith unto the churches.

THE FORCES OF SATAN—SO IN THE NATURAL; SO IN THE SPIRITUAL

Forces – in a military point of view it is applied to army, fortification, etc.

Principality – the territory of a reigning prince, or one who gives to a prince a title of courtesy, powers or powerful influences, as celestial or demonic powers. Paul used this term when referring to angels and demons who were invested with power. (Rom. 8:38, 1Cor. 15:24, Eph. 1:21; 3:10; 6:12; Col. 1:16, 2:10, 15; Tit. 3:1)

Territorial Jurisdiction – the sovereign jurisdiction exercised by a state over all land, waters, persons and properties within boundaries.

Powers – ability of performing, belongs essentially to God, who is All-powerful, the Omnipotent. One power has the sense of: ability, strength, right, privilege, or dignity, absolute authority, the exertion or act of power, as of the Holy Ghost, exercise control or dominion.

Legion – a great number of multitude, equivalent to our regiment, but comprise a much larger number of men (3,000 to 6,000 men).

Regiment, battalion, squadron, brigade - company, troop, team, detail, unit, task force.

Dignities – persons higher in honor probably angels as being spiritual beings of preeminent dignity. 2 Pet. 2:10.

Dominion – the fourth part of the hierarchy of heavenly beings; also called dominions, sovereign authority, the right of absolute possession and use, ownership.

Stronghold – a place in an individual's life that Satan has lodged and strongly defends

Prince of Persia – the angel of darkness that represented the Persian world power, to which Israel was then subject.

HOW DOES SATAN RULE IN THE EARTH?

He has an army of demons or evil spirits organized in a hierarchy of demonic power structures dependent on the power of Satan's stronghold over the world system. These demons are ranked in the principalities and are set in order as our armed forces are...*so in the natural; so in the spiritual.* Satan is neither omnipotent nor omnipresent, therefore, he works through a host of unclean spirits or demons (Luke 8:27, 29) that influence, manipulate, and control the structural powers.

When these demons are dispersed into the world, they bring confusion and chaos. They seek to neutralize any potential threats to their control. They frustrate attempts to reform the structural powers by hardening their resistance to change, thus producing rebellion against God, evil and oppression.

This structure is categorized into these divisions: geopolitical, geographic and territorial powers.

Below is a list of demonic ranks, as it relates to the spiritual:

a. *World rulers* or *rulers of this age* (Eph 6:12) are the highest order of powers directly under Satan. These demons were involved in the most critical confrontation of all—the death of Christ (John 14:30).

b. *Principalities*, *princedoms* or *rulerships* are powers over territories. These demonic powers watch over the nations. Examples are the Prince of Persia and the Prince of Greece (Dan 10:13, 20).

c. *Rulers* (Col 1:16, Eph 1:21, 3:10) are the more numerous and lower orders who are over specific regions, cities or territories.

d. *Dominions* or *lordships* are demonic officers over particular cultural and social areas of influence. (i.e. political, educational, philosophical ideologies, media, legal system, music, entertainment and the arts, etc.)

e. *Powers* (Rom 8:38; 1Pet 3:22) are a multiplicity of controlling powers over specific institutions great and small (e.g. business corporations, educational establishments, welfare organizations, governing bodies, societies, clubs and associations of all kinds)

f. *Authorities* (Col 2:15, Eph 3:10) are beings with the right, delegated to them from above, to exercise authority and to represent a power source and act on its behalf.

g. *Spiritual forces or the spiritual realm* (Eph 6:12) relate particularly to activity in the realm of spirit such as false prophecy, false religion, the occult, witchcraft, magic, heretical doctrine, lying wonders, deceiving signs and counterfeit miracles.

Below is a list of military ranks and levels, as it relates to the natural:

a. **General** – Superior in rank, next above a Lieutenant General, equivalent to an Admiral
Levels – General, Brigadier General, Lieutenant General, Major General

b. **Lieutenant General** – an officer ranking next above a Major General and next below a General

c. **Major General** – an officer commanding a division of an Air Force command, in ranking next above a Brigadier General and next below a Lieutenant General.

d. **Brigadier General** – an officer commanding a brigade or a wing, ranking next above a colonel and next below a major general

e. **Lieutenant** – a commissioned officer that fills the place of a superior in the absence or acts for him under his direction
Levels – Lieutenant, Lieutenant Commander, First Lieutenant, Second Lieutenant, Lieutenant (Junior Grade)

f. **First Lieutenant** - a commissioned officer ranking next below a Captain

g. **Lieutenant Commander** – a commissioned officer in the Navy

h. **Lieutenant** – a commissioned officer in the Navy ranking below the Lieutenant Commander

i. **Lieutenant (Junior Grade)** – a commissioned officer in the Navy ranking next above an Ensign

j. **Lieutenant Governor** – an officer authorized to perform the duties of a governor during his absence or disability, or take the place in case of death or resignation

k. **Major** – an Army officer in the ranking next above a Captain and next below a Lieutenant Colonel

l. **Captain** – a commissioned officer of the third rank in the Army; a commissioned officer of the sixth rank in the Navy, above a First Lieutenant and below a Major, entitled to command a warship, equal to a Colonel

m. **Colonel** – a commissioned officer of the sixth rank. Ranking next above a Lieutenant Colonel and next below a Brigadier General, whose proper command is a regiment.

> *Levels – Colonel, Lieutenant Colonel*

n. **Lieutenant Colonel** – a commissioned officer of the fifth rank acts as an understudy or assistant to a Colonel in commanding a regiment, or is himself in control of a battalion or squadron, ranking next above a Major and next below a Colonel

o. **Sergeant** – a non-commissioned military officer ranking next above a Corporal
   Levels – Sergeant, Sergeant Major, Sergeant at Arms

p. **Sergeant Major** – the principal enlisted assistant to the adjutant of a battalion or higher unit in the Army, the highest non-commissioned officer in the Marine Corps.

q. **Sergeant-at-Arms** – An executive officer in a legislative body who enforces order

r. **Corporal** - a non-commissioned officer of the fifth grade, commanding a squad, and ranking next above a Private, first class, and next below a Sergeant, formerly in the Navy, a senior petty officer who attended to police matters under the Master at Arms.

Levels - Corporal, Lance Corporal, Corporal's Guard

s. **Lance Corporal** – a private soldier acting as Corporal.

t. **Corporal's Guard** – the squad of men detailed for guard or other duty under a corporal.

u. **Master of Arms** – a petty officer that maintains discipline and order on a naval vessel.

v. **Ensign** – a commissioned officer in the Navy of the lowest grade ranking with a Second Lieutenant in the Army.

w. **Private** – a soldier
Levels – Private, Private First Class

x. **Private First Class** – a soldier ranking next above a Private and below a Corporal

WEAPONS OF OUR WARFARE

Rebuke – to reprove sharply, admonish, reprimand, a strong and authoritative expression of disapproval

Contend – dispute, fight, battle, struggle, argue, try to win

Prayer – communion with God and recognition of his presence, the act of offering reverent petitions to God in the name of Jesus, request, entreaty, supplication.

Fasting – to abstain from food beyond the usual time; to go without food wholly or in part

WHAT AUTHORITY DO WE HAVE WHEN SATAN'S POWERS ARE IN OPERATION?

At an early age we are taught the Pledge of Allegiance to the Flag. Although the words *...one nation under God, indivisible with liberty and justice for all* are stated, it makes me wonder which "god;" for there are many. Even on our dollar bills we read the words "In God We Trust". The bible says that God is a spirit and they that worship Him must worship Him in spirit and in truth (John 4:24). Therefore, if we observe the acts of this government and its leaders, one would assume that the *god* of this nation is Satan. This is evident with the removal of prayer from morning devotions in public schools to the acceptance of witchcraft and Satanism disguised behind Halloween. The abortion of innocent babies is being committed every day but is disguised behind a woman's right and as a form of birth control. The acceptance of homosexuality is at its highest in the government, school system, workplace and even churches.

Scripture teaches us that the weapons we use to fight Satan are not carnal but mighty through God to the pulling down of strongholds (2Cor. 10:4). If this is true, then Michael, the archangel, would have responded to Satan in a different manner than he did according to Daniel Chapter 10 and Jude verse nine. Although Michael, being one of the chief princes of God, was a special guardian to the Jews in their time of trouble, he respected authority. During the time of Daniel's prayer, Daniel's words were heard the first day, but God's messenger was detained on the way by the opposition of the powers of darkness. The angel of the Lord did not come until three weeks after Daniel had prayed because he was detained by the angel of the Persian rulers to contend for Israel. Without the help of Michael, who helped influence the Persian king to permit the Jews' return to Jerusalem, he would not have gotten free.

Another confrontation Michael had with the forces of Satan is when he contended with the devil over the body of Moses. He made it very clear that he did not have a personal vendetta against the devil so by contending for Moses body in the name of the Lord gained Michael this victory (...the Lord rebuke thee. Jude, verse 9).

The power of the cross was never realized by Satan until it was too late. None of the rulers of this age understood it, for if they had they would not have crucified the Lord of glory (1Cor 2:8). But God...

God's purpose in redemption is two-fold:

(1) To restore all creation to its original state, under the headship of Christ (Eph 1:10)

(2) To transform creation as the arena of the Father's glory in the age to come (Rom 8:21, Habuk 2:14).

Jesus' death cancelled the destructive power of sin and the punishment of the law that was against us. His resurrection robbed Satan and destroyed his strongest weapon against us, the power of death (Heb 2:14). *Destroy,* in the Greek (*katargeo),* literally means *to reduce to inactivity,* thus *abolish, disarm, render power-less* or *nullify.* Jesus effectively exposed, stripped, and unmasked the forces of Satan. He disarmed the principalities and powers of the darkness of this world (Col 2:15). Jesus has established His authority over both the demonic and the structural powers (eternal and temporal, spiritual and secular; Matt 28:18). His ultimate obedience exhausted Satan's powers. In the end, death had to yield to this obedience and Christ rose triumphantly, taking the keys to death, hell and the grave from Satan. Hallelujah!

We have authority in the Name of Jesus and by the Blood of the Lamb to pursue our enemies, overtake them, and consume them. In Israel's history, the outcome of a war depended entirely on the kings. In the Old Testament, during countless times of war, Israel's kings would seek the Lord for instruction. The kings knew that they must acknowledge the spiritual power that decided victory or defeat. Once the kings' souls was filled with victory before the battle, the actual outcome of the battle was the manifestation that the real victory or defeat already existed (Ps 18:32-34, 1Kings 20:13). Our final victory in spiritual warfare with the forces of Satan is ultimately assured because Jesus Christ, our King, has total victory in His soul (1Cor 15:25-28). Real victory already exists for the believer, and the outcome of our battles is the outward manifestation of what is already in Christ. Therefore, the victory that is in Christ must penetrate our heart and soul so that His victory becomes ours (1 John 4:4, 5:4).

Conclusion

Prayer and fasting are spiritual weapons that are imperatively used by believers in Christ to break, shatter, and destroy the powers of Satan. God's counsel confuses and dissolves the enemy's counsel, so that the enemy's will is weakened and paralyzed, and his plan cannot take effect.

WAYS TO CONDUCT A SPIRITUAL BATTLE

1. Remember that God is in control of the battle. He directs the campaign and determines the strategy.

2. There must be a sacrifice of worship, praise, and thanksgiving to the Lord. The purpose of our spiritual warfare is the restoration of worship, thus, reversing Satan's rebellion, and reasserting God's rightful place as Creator; and man's rightful place as a worshipper.

3. Remember not to bite off more than you can chew. Take care of only what has been measured to you from God. Nobody else can, or will, do what you are required of God to do. It's not by power, nor by might, but by the Spirit of the Lord that you carry out His instructions. So do it!

4. Learn to use the prophetic Word of God as it is quickened by the Holy Spirit in you.

5. Speak the judgment Word of God against the demonic powers. Hold the commands of God with your spiritual will against the will of your flesh.

6. Declare to the powers the greatness, majesty, holiness, and victory of Christ, in order to weaken and terrify them.

7. Discern the critical issues of God's timing.

8. Locate the enemy's limitations; there you will find his weaknesses. Seize the moment when it is time.

9. Wait on the proceeding word from God to "Pursue, Overtake and Consume" your enemy (Josh 2:5).

10. Understand the law of occupation and the power principle "Preparation Precedes Blessings". Once God has given you the command to take the land, you must have the proper resources in order to hold or occupy that specific territory. If you are not prepared; the wild beasts will multiply and you could lose all. (Deut 7:22).

LESSON REVIEW

1. There is an _____ that is set in the earth as well as in the heavens.

2. Name the three responsibilities that man has been given regarding dominion over the earth.

3. Satan has authority to be ruler of this _____, and prince of the _____ of the _____.

4. What is compromise?

5. What does pride breed?

6. Name three ways to conduct a spiritual battle?

Scripture References:

Ephesians 6:12; 1:10,21; 3:10
Matthew 25:34-45; 2:16; 28:18
Genesis 1:28
Romans 8:21-22,38; 5:20
Psalms 37:23
Exodus 1:22
1 Samuel 28:7; 15
Daniel 4:25,35,37; 10:13,20
Proverbs 14:34

The Day I Got Set Free

MY DIARY OF DELIVERANCE

The weapons of our warfare are not carnal, but mighty through God to the pulling down of strongholds. (1 Cor. 10:4)

Date: _____

- ❑ Monday
- ❑ Tuesday
- ❑ Wednesday
- ❑ Thursday
- ❑ Friday
- ❑ Saturday
- ❑ Sunday

If two of you shall agree on earth as touching any thing that they shall ask, it shall be done for them. (Matthew 18:19)

Today Lord I set myself in agreement with Bishop George Bloomer and the mighty prayer warriors of Bethel Family Worship Center that this yoke will be destroyed in my life, in Jesus' name. Amen

_____

_____

_____

_____

_____

_____

_____

_____

_____

_____

_____

_____

_____

_____

_____

_____

_____

_____

_____

_____

_____

_____

_____

_____

_____

LESSON 5: Demonology and Governments

_____

_____

_____

_____

_____

_____

_____

_____

_____

_____

_____

_____

_____

_____

_____

_____

_____

_____

_____

_____

_____

_____

_____

_____

_____

_____

_____

_____

_____

_____

_____

_____

_____

_____

_____

_____

_____

LESSON

DEVICES OF SATAN

Lest Satan should get an advantage of us: for we are not ignorant of his devices.

—2 Corinthians 2:11

INTRODUCTION

Solomon informs us that *the fear of the LORD is the beginning of knowledge but fools despise wisdom and instruction* (Proverbs 1:7). Do you fear the Lord or are you a fool? The first step in knowing Satan's devices is to establish relationship with God, and His Son Jesus Christ, and then declare it to the principalities.

Prayer

Lord Jesus,

We thank You for showing us the devices of Satan. We know his tricks now and can see him coming. Equip us to defeat his cause, in Jesus' name. Amen.

LESSON

Knowledge - A result or product of knowing information (i.e. data, facts, specifics, details) or understanding acquired through experience, practical ability or skill.

Omniscience - The divine attribute of perfect knowledge. Perfect knowledge of

God is exclusively His attribute. It relates to Himself and to all beyond Himself. It includes all things that are actual and all things that are possible.

Ignorance - The condition of not being informed, having a lack of knowledge, an act, offense, or sin due to ignorance. The term implies error, going astray. 516 (Ungers) Greek- *want of knowledge.*

Transgression - Used synonymously with sin, as indicating a violation of the law through ignorance (*sin of omission*). All sin is transgression but all transgression is not sin.

IGNORANCE IS NOT BLISS!

Many believe that being ignorant to a given situation, or sin, exempts one from suffering the consequences that accompany the act of sin, but this is not true. The Bible teaches that *the soul that sinneth, it shall die* (Ezekiel 18:20). There are many people who have done things in ignorance and paid for it dearly. And there are some who have done things in ignorance and suffered nothing. But, if you sin against the Lord, *be sure your sin will find you out* (Numbers 32:23). The Old Testament teaches us about sins that were committed in ignorance. When a soul committed a sin in ignorance, the priest that was anointed would kill a young bullock that was without blemish and sacrifice it unto the Lord as a sin offering. When the whole congregation of Israel transgressed the law of God in ignorance, the elders of the congregation would kill a bullock, and the priest would make atonement for them for forgiveness of sin. Whether these sins committed were done in ignorance individually or collectively, a penalty for the sin had to be executed—the shedding of innocent blood was required.

In the New Testament scriptures, Acts Chapter 17, we see how God deals with *this ignorance* (verse 30). The Apostle Paul stands in the midst of Mars Hill and tells the men of Athens that the objects of their worship indicated that they were very religious, but they did not know the only True and Living God—evidenced by an altar with an inscription "TO THE UNKNOWN GOD." Can a person worship God without knowing Him? Jesus says in John 4:24 that *God is a Spirit: and they that worship him, must worship him in spirit and in truth.* The hypocrites, or pretenders, (according to Isaiah 29:13) draw unto the Lord with their mouths and honor Him with their lips, but their hearts are far from God. *In vain they worship God ...teaching for doctrines the commandments of men* (Mark 7:7). At one time God did overlook (or wink at) *times of ignorance* but NOW He

commandeth all men everywhere to repent
(Acts 17:30).

Also in Acts Chapter Three, Peter and John
deal with the sinful ignorance of the people. At
the gate of the temple called Beautiful, through
the power of God, they heal a lame man and
the crowd marveled at this miracle. But Peter
reproved them, and preached Christ crucified,
and compelled them to repent and be convert-
ed, *that their sin be blotted out* (Acts 3:19).
What was their sin? When Jesus hung on
Calvary's cross, He prayed to the Father,
Forgive them; for they know not what they do
(Luke 23:34). Through moral blindness, they
denied Jesus, the Christ and delivered Him up
to be crucified. (Howbeit God revealed through
the mouth of His prophets that Christ would
suffer.) Jesus *Christ hath redeemed us from
the curse of the law being made a curse for us*
(Galatians 3:13). He who knew no sin became
sin for us *that we might be made the righteousness of God in him* (2 Corinthians 6:21).
Therefore we no longer deem it necessary to
sacrifice a bullock or lamb for a sin offering.
Jesus is the Sacrificial Lamb who has taken
away the sin of the world (John 1:29).

FIRST STEP: *BREAKTHROUGH FROM THE DEVICES OF SATAN—TRUE REPENTANCE*

1. **Satan** – Lucifer (light bearer), Beelzebul (Baal is prince), diabolos, father of lies, deceiver, accuser of the brethren, tempter, thief, roaring lion, evil one, the destroyer, the enemy, dragon, angel of light, ruler of this world, prince of the air, old serpent, defeated foe

2. **Devices** – strategy, tactic, line of attack, scheme, method, plan, procedure

3. **Repentance** – 918 (Ungers)-M*etanoia (Greek)*, a change of mind. A thorough change in the hearts of men from sin and toward God. A genuine sorrow toward God on account of sin. Humble self-surrender to the will and service of God. Although faith alone is the condition of salvation repentance is bound up with faith and inseparable from it. There can be no saving faith without true repentance.

4. **Salvation** – freely offered to all of mankind but is conditioned upon repentance and faith in Christ Jesus. Proceeds from the love of God. Based upon the atonement wrought by Christ as realized in forgiveness, regeneration, sanctification, culmination in the resurrection and glorification of all true believers.

There is no excuse! Whether we commit sin in ignorance or not, we must render true repentance to God. In Acts 2:38... *Then Peter said unto them, Repent, and be baptized every one of you in the name of Jesus Christ for the remission of sins, and ye shall receive the gift of the Holy Ghost. If thou shalt confess with thy mouth the Lord Jesus, and shalt believe in thine heart that God hath raised him from the dead, thou shalt be saved* (Romans 10:9). Putting on the new man (Ephesians 4:24; Colossians 3:10) is manifest in your daily living. Your former conversation – the old man (Ephesians 4:22) – is now crucified with Christ (Galatians 2:19). *If any man be in Christ, he is a new creature: old things are passed away; behold, all things are become new* (2 Corinthians 5:17). This is a familiar scripture and many of us quote it quite fluently, but how many of us daily put away the old man? Because it is a process, this is not done overnight. Satan knows this and strategically sets traps to tempt us. Most of us are not honest with ourselves. We hide behind masks and pretend to be someone whom we are not. We talk the talk but we can't walk the walk because it is a process. Be open and honest with yourself, God, and others. This is a daily walk. We all mature in the faith. Seek God's will for your life.

SECOND STEP: *IDENTIFYING THE DEVICES OF SATAN—BY THE WORD OF GOD*

The Bible teaches us the whole story from creation, to man's fall, to redemption through the blood of Jesus Christ, to the last enemy destroyed. We, as believers of Christ, know how the story ends but many of us don't know where the pitfalls of Satan are placed to keep us from our purpose and destiny. Because of the cunning ingenuity of the forces of darkness, our ignorance keeps us unprepared and uninformed of the battle we are to fight against his dark forces. Consequently, we continue living defeated lives, thereby not fulfilling the ministry to which God has called us. That's why it is so important to identify the devices of Satan. And the only way to know this is to daily embrace God's Word.

Second Timothy 2:15 says: *Study to show thyself approved unto God, a workman that needeth not to be ashamed, rightly dividing the word of truth.* We have become too busy to study God's Word on a daily basis. *The care of this world, the deceitfulness of riches,* (and the lusts of other things) *choke the Word* of God (Matthew 13:22), so that when affliction or persecution arises, we are easily offended. Therefore, we are defenseless against the craftiness and subtleties of Satan. As believers, our key defense against Satan is to be able to detect his persistent effort to gain advantage over us by being watchful of his strategies.

What devices can Satan use to prevent us from seeking God?

1. **Unforgiveness**
2. **Pride of Life**
3. **Lust of the flesh**

❏ THE DEVICE – UNFORGIVENESS

Unforgiveness is a big hindrance to our relationship with God. Some of us cannot forgive ourselves because Satan reminds us of our past mistakes. We hold grudges against those who are responsible for the hurts of the past and present. Unforgiveness is a tool, which Satan uses to keep us separated from God. Although Satan is notorious for misquoting God's Word, he knows that if we do not forgive our brother's trespasses then God cannot forgive us (Matthew 18:35). And if we do not forgive ourselves, then we will not repent; and if we do not repent, then God cannot forgive us. God gives us authority to release ourselves and other individuals from the bondage of unforgiveness. *Whatsoever ye shall bind on earth shall be bound in heaven: and whatsoever ye shall loose on earth shall be loosed in heaven* (Matthew 18:18). Paul encourages us to forgive each other lest Satan get an advantage of us (2 Corinthians 2:10-11)

□ THE DEVICE - PRIDE OF LIFE

There is a way which seemeth right unto a man, but the end thereof are the ways of death (Proverbs 14:12, 16:25). Therefore walk NOT in the vanity of your mind (Ephesians 4:17) where pride lurks. Pride is puffed up, all knowing, self righteous and governed by the flesh. Many civilizations have fallen because of pride. Many homes have been broken because of pride. Many souls have been lost because of pride. Pride comes before a fall (Proverbs 16:28). One of the ways to see if you are full of pride is to ask these questions:

1. Can I be corrected or admonished?
2. Can I listen and learn from someone else?
3. Do I look down on people of low estate?
4. Do I try to keep up with the Jones's?
5. Do I do whatever it takes to have fame and fortune?

It is understood that we should take pride in ourselves, our family, things we own, and so on, but there must be a balance. Where many have fallen, however, is in the vanity of their minds, *which is corrupt according to the deceitful lusts* (Ephesians 4:22). Their understanding is darkened to the life of God in Christ because of the blindness of their hearts (Ephesians 4:18). What a man thinketh in his heart so is he (Proverbs 23:7). So then if you are seeking worldly lusts, and not the things of God, you will squash whoever gets in your way. Knowing God's Word is far greater than acquiring temporal things of the earth. Your level of reasoning, compassion, respect and care for others will diminish. The Bible teaches us to store our treasures in heaven and not on the earth *where moth and rust doth corrupt, or where thieves break through and steal. For where your treasure is, there will your heart be also.* (Matthew 6:20-21) It is necessary to make plans in life, but it is wise to be led by God and His Holy Spirit. Repent and walk humbly before your God. Seek Him daily. *Trust in the Lord with all thine heart; and lean not unto thine own understanding. In all thy ways acknowledge him, and he shall direct thy paths* (Proverbs 3:5,6).

□ **THE DEVICE - LUST OF THE FLESH**

Just because it sounds good, feels good, and tastes good, does not constitute that it is right for you. Because everyone else is doing it does not constitute that it is right. James 1:14-15 speaks on being drawn away from God and enticed by our own lust. However, we blame the devil or someone else when we want to do what we want to do. Once lust is conceived, it brings forth sin, and when sin is finished it brings forth death (James 1:15).

If we are not prayed up, we will fulfill the lust of the flesh; according to Galatians 5:19-21: –

[19]Now the works of the flesh are manifest, which are these: Adultery, Fornication, Uncleanness, Lasciviousness,
[20]Idolatry, Witchcraft, Hatred, Variance, Emulations, Wrath, Strife, Seditions, Heresies,
[21]Envyings, Murders, Drunkenness, Revelings, and such like: of the which I tell you before, as I have also told you in time past, that they which do such things shall not inherit the kingdom of God.

These practices are done through disobedience to God's Word.

Can Christians commit such acts?   Yes!

ARE YOU WALKING IN THE FLESH?

Consider these things:

1. I don't have a clear conscience. I feel regretful, ashamed, and/or guilty.
2. I rationalize, justify, and make excuses.
3. I cover up, hide, pretend, and remain in a state of denial.
4. I pilfer, lie, deceive.

Now if we deny *ungodliness and worldly lusts, we* shall *live soberly, righteously, and godly, in this present world* (Titus 2:12), because perplexity, anxiety, frustration, loneliness, boredom, doubt, fear, stress, anger, and regret will invade our lives at times. The key is denying the flesh and the oppression of despair and discouragement that war against our faith in God.

[3]*For though we walk in the flesh,* (live in this life) *we do not war after the flesh:*
[4](*For the weapons of our warfare are not carnal, but mighty through God to the pulling down of strong holds;)*
[5]*Casting down imaginations and every high thing that exalteth itself against the knowledge of God, and bringing into captivity every thought to the obedience of Christ.*
—2 Corinthians 10:3-5

When we walk in the Spirit, we will not fulfill the lust of the flesh (Galatians 5:16). Therefore, put on love, joy, peace, goodness, gentleness, faith, long suffering, meekness, temperance, patience, because against these things there is no law (Galatians 5:22-23).

WHAT ABOUT SPIRITUAL DISCERNMENT?

The activities of demons can be detected separately from the gift of discernment. Discernment is the detecting of the thoughts and intents of the heart by the Spirit of God, whether they are good or bad. It is not the ability to identify the sicknesses of individuals. That is the word of knowledge. One only has to know Satan's nature and actions, as discussed in the previous chapter, in order to discern. Some of his characteristics include:

1. A LIAR
   Satan is a liar, and his nature is to work and deceive.

2. MURDERER
   Satan is the reason for death coming into the world. From the very beginning, and throughout the ages, he has sought to destroy mankind.

3. A THIEF
   John 10:10: *The thief cometh not but for to steal, and to kill, and to destroy: I am come that they might have life, and that they might have it more abundantly.*

Anything contrary to the Word of God can be listed as the work of demons. It does not take spiritual discernment to detect these.

Conclusion

It is not easy for God's people to detect and cast out demons because most churches have not taught people how to detect, recognize or exert power over demons.

In 2 Corinthians 2:11, Paul writes, *Lest Satan should get an advantage of us; for we are not ignorant of his devices.*
Due to a lack of knowledge, many believers have been ignorant in the area of spiritual warfare. In few instances do they know when they are being attacked, nor do they know how to react when they do recognize an attack, because the attention of believers has been more on material than spiritual things. The truth of the matter is that many believers don't want to talk about the devil or how he is operating in the church. If you do not expose him for who he is from the Word of God, and if you do not apply the truth from God's Word to defeat him, you will never know your enemy.

There is no excuse for not seeking to know the Word of God, for it is the knowledge of God's Word that prevents Satan from using his devices to wrap, tie and entangle us over and over again. *Stand fast therefore in the liberty wherewith Christ hath made us free, and be not entangled again with the yoke of bondage* (Galatians 5:1). Invite discipline into your daily living. Solomon says that *the fear of the Lord is the beginning of knowledge: but fools despise wisdom and instruction* (Proverbs 1:7). Don't be a fool but be wise. *And with all thy getting get understanding* (Proverbs 4:7). Set aside time with God for worship and praise. Read and meditate on the Word of God, and use it when the enemy comes. Develop a strong relationship with Christ through prayer and fasting. Continue in fellowship with other believers in the household of faith.

Know this: You have purpose and destiny, but you must keep your mind renewed daily in Christ to walk in the newness of life. *Forgetting those things which are behind, and reaching forth unto those things which are before, I press toward the mark for the prize of the high calling of God in Christ Jesus* (Philippians 3:13-14). Through His Spirit, God will begin to reveal His truths to you. He will perfect you and stir up the gift that lies dormant within you. So, *when the enemy shall come in like a flood, the Spirit of the Lord shall lift up a standard against him* (Isaiah 59:19).

****

LESSON REVIEW

1. Whether we commit sin in ignorance or not, we must render true _____ to God.

2. The only way to identify the devices of Satan is to daily embrace God's _____.

3. Name three devices of Satan.

4. Name the three things that choke the Word of God, and give the scripture reference.

5. If we do not forgive ourselves, then we will not _____; and if we do not _____, then God cannot _____ us.

The Day I Got Set Free

My Diary of Deliverance

The weapons of our warfare are not carnal, but mighty through God to the pulling down of strongholds. (1 Cor. 10:4)

Date: _____

- ☐ Monday
- ☐ Tuesday
- ☐ Wednesday
- ☐ Thursday
- ☐ Friday
- ☐ Saturday
- ☐ Sunday

**If two of you shall agree on earth as touching any thing that they shall ask, it shall be done for them. (Matthew 18:19)

Today Lord I set myself in agreement with Bishop George Bloomer and the mighty prayer warriors of Bethel Family Worship Center that this yoke will be destroyed in my life, in Jesus' name. Amen

_____

_____

_____

_____

LESSON 6: Devices of Satan

_____

_____

_____

_____

_____

_____

_____

_____

_____

_____

_____

_____

_____

_____

_____

_____

_____

_____

_____

LESSON 6: Devices of Satan

_____

_____

_____

_____

_____

_____

_____

_____

_____

_____

_____

_____

_____

_____

_____

_____

_____

_____

LESSON

OPPRESSION, DEPRESSION, POSSESSION

Be sober, be vigilant, because your adversary, the devil, as a roaring lion, walketh about seeking whom he may devour. —1 Peter 5:8

INTRODUCTION

God's plan is to redeem and restore man to perfect standing with Him, so that man can have abundant life in the earth and eternal life in heavenly places. On the other hand, Satan and his demons are commissioned to destroy the souls of men, and render them to eternal damnation. Why then would Satan devote all of his time to frustrate and humiliate the children of God when his enemy is God? He knows that he is eternally defeated, and any further attempts by him to come against God would be useless. So instead, he attacks God's most loved creation—mankind. Satan sends his demons to attack through three avenues:

1. **Oppression**
2. **Depression**
3. **Demonic Possession**

Prayer

Lord Jesus,

Thank You for allowing us to know the vehicles through which Satan attacks. Now our discernment will not only come from past experiences, but from the things which we have learned here. Amen.

LESSON

Oppression 1. a) Unjust or cruel exercise of authority or power b) something that oppresses, especially in an unjust or excessive exercise of power
2. A sense of being weighed down in body or mind: *depression*

Depression 1. A state of feeling sad: DEJECTION
2. A psychoneurotic or psychotic disorder marked by sadness, inactivity, difficulty in thinking and concentration, a significant increase or decrease in appetite and time spent sleeping, feelings of dejection and hopelessness, and sometimes suicidal tendencies.

Possession 1. a) The act of having or taking into control b)control or occupancy of property without regard to ownership
2. Domination by something (as an evil spirit, a passion, or an idea) b) a psychological state in which an individual's normal personality is replaced by another

Isaiah 14:12-16 tells us of Satan's plan to ascend into heaven above the throne of God, but instead, he and one-third of the angels (fallen angels) were cast down from heaven to earth to await their final destination—hell. The judgement of God has already fallen upon Satan, and he knows that he is no match for God. Instead, he orchestrates attacks on God's prized creation, mankind, by dispatching demons to all parts of the earth with orders *to steal, to kill, and to destroy* (John 10:10). Satan cannot destroy the plan of God, but he can hinder the progress of mankind's faith in God.

SATAN'S PURPOSE: Satan's purpose is to frustrate God's plan of redemption.

Whatever tactic Satan uses, his plan is to drag every soul he possibly can to hell, in an effort to spite God's Plan. He is after you!

*But the Word of God says:

24The LORD of hosts hath sworn, saying, Surely as I have thought, so shall it come to pass; and as I have purposed, so shall it stand:
26This is the purpose that is purposed upon the whole earth: and this is the hand that is stretched out upon all the nations.

[27]For the LORD of hosts hath purposed, and who shall disannul it? and his hand is stretched out; and who shall turn it back?
—Isaiah 14:24,26,27

SATAN'S DEMONIC TRIO OF PROGRESSIVE INSANITY

1. OPPRESSION –

We know, and Satan knows that his ultimate destination is hell. Meanwhile, his plan is to oppress and destroy as many lives as possible. Oppression is like a weight. It carries with it a spirit of illusion that clouds the mind and confuses the thinking, causing individuals to stray and wander without direction and purpose. Under the spirit of oppression, fear sets in as a masquerading defense, setting the individual up for a total shutdown. In other words, Satan has taken authority over the person, enslaving him or her in cruel, unjust bondage. Those who succumb to this emotional ploy are totally unaware of fear's masquerade, and are further lured into the deceptive clutches of Satan. It is at this stage that Satan lunges in for the kill! Meanwhile, his victim doesn't even realize what is hitting him. This spirit will present a struggle between the will of God and the will of man, pulling down and ultimately suffocating the life out of the individual. Only the individual's willingness to invoke God's power can set him or her free.

> And it came to pass on the morrow, that the evil spirit from God came upon Saul, and he prophesied in the midst of the house: and David played with his hand, as at other times: and there was a javelin in Saul's hand.
> And Saul cast the javelin; for he said, I will smite David even to the wall with it. And David avoided out of his presence twice.
> And Saul was afraid of David, because the LORD was with him, and was departed from Saul.
> —1 Samuel 18:10-12

King Saul was oppressed by an evil spirit. But the power of God, through the music of David, overwhelmed the spirit, saving David's life.

OTHER MANIFESTATIONS OF OPPRESSION

Oppression may be manifested through sickness as in Mark 9: 17 –27, where a father brought his son to Jesus because he had a dumb spirit. And the scripture goes on to say, *And wheresoever he taketh him, he teareth him: and he foameth, and gnasheth with his teeth, and pineth away: ..., and they brought him unto him: and when he saw him,* *straightway the spirit tare him; and he fell on the ground, and wallowed foaming. And he asked his father, How long is it ago since this came unto him? And he said, Of a child..*

Again in Luke 13:10-13, *...And behold, there was a woman which had a spirit of infirmity eighteen years, and was bowed together, and could in no wise lift up herself.*

Oppression may be manifested in any type of habit that a person finds difficulty in breaking. This could include not only sexual lust, but a lust for money, power, tobacco, alcohol, and so on.

Unfortunately, many times the oppressed Christian decides within himself that he can no longer go on under the heaviness of oppression he is forced to endure. Rather than continue fighting what the enemy has convinced him is "a losing battle," he gives up and gives in to the sinful drives of the flesh.

This is why Proverbs 4:23 admonishes: *Keep (guard) your heart with all diligence.* It is important to guard our hearts so that even when Satan's attacks surface, and the mind has been clouded by frustration, he still can't reach the spirit. If man's spirit can be oppressed, destruction not only is knocking at the door, it is destined to take place–unless the individual becomes wise and invokes God's power to finally be set free.

Oppression Has Many Names

Some of the names of oppression include:
1. Boredom
2. Loneliness
3. Alienation
4. Criticism
5. Racism
6. Arrogance

Boredom and Loneliness – can normally be satisfied by the company of others, but when one is oppressed by demonic forces, a person can be in a crowded room and still feel the heaviness of boredom and loneliness.

Other oppressive spirits are acquired through a spirit of transfer—bad seeds planted by an oppressor, past traumas, bad teaching, listening to complaints and problems of others on a consistent basis, and so on.

HOW TO DEFEAT OPPRESSION

Plain and simple, James 4:7 tells us that if we resist the devil, he will flee. The spirits of depression and oppression can only be destroyed through prayer and resistance. Once an individual succumbs to the chronic forces of oppression and depression, the final stage is Satan's possession and destruction.

2. DEPRESSION –

Oppression joins forces with depression to collapse its victim's world. Though depression is looked upon as a mental illness and chemical imbalance, we as Christians know that it is a demon. Medication doesn't provide deliverance, and in many cases, it even produces adverse effects. This is not to say, however, that if you are currently taking medication for depression that you should stop, but as a Christian, you must not be afraid to confront the demon of depression, and exercise your God-given power of initiating his defeat. Depression causes worry, doubt, and unbelief; therefore it cannot be pampered, but one must hear from God in order to combat this evil and deadly force.

> [1]*In those days was Hezekiah sick unto death. And Isaiah the prophet the son of Amoz came unto him, and said unto him, Thus saith the LORD, Set thine house in order: for thou shalt die, and not live.*
> [2]*Then Hezekiah turned his face toward the wall, and prayed unto the LORD.*

³And said, Remember now, O LORD, I beseech thee, how I have walked before thee in truth, and with a perfect heart, and have done that which is good in thy sight. And Hezekiah wept sore.
⁴Then came the word of the LORD to Isaiah saying,
⁵Go and say to Hezekiah, Thus saith the LORD, the God of David thy father, I have heard thy prayer, I have seen thy tears: behold, I will add unto thy days fifteen years.
¹⁴Like a crane or a swallow, so did I chatter: I did mourn as a dove: mine eyes fail with looking upward: O LORD, I am oppressed; undertake for me.

—Isaiah 38:1-5,14

Hezekiah was a good king. He loved the Lord, and was extremely prosperous because of his obedience to God's commands. When he first took over the throne of his kingdom, he cleansed the temple of all ungodliness. He even taught the people to worship and to give offerings in the atmosphere of worship. The entire atmosphere of his kingdom changed, and the Bible likened it to the times of Solomon. However, Hezekiah later became proud and lifted up in his heart. He did not repay according to the favor that was shown unto him (2 Chronicles 32:25). The wrath of God was upon him and his kingdom, Judah and Jerusalem. They must have sensed it (probably due to their consistent lifestyle of worship under Hezekiah's leadership) because they all repented before God, and the anger was lifted—they were forgiven. But before they all repented, Hezekiah became sick unto the point of death. The prophet Isaiah told him that he would surely die. Hezekiah was overwhelmed in spirit by this tragic news. He prayed intensely that God would change the outcome. He wept sorely before the Lord, and told the Lord that he was oppressed (Isaiah 38:14). He also told God that he was in mourning, referring to depression, like a dove. You see, the word "mourn" means "to grieve." When you look up the word "grieve," it states: "sorrow or mental suffering resulting from loss, affliction, regret, etc.; physical pain; distress." So, Hezekiah's oppression had intensified itself by bringing in its partner, depression. If God didn't take his life, the partners of oppression and depression alone could have killed him. The prophet Isaiah later returned with an answer from the Lord: God was going to allow Hezekiah to live. With just that word from the Lord, Hezekiah rejoiced and gave thanksgiving to God. His health was restored, and God added fifteen years to his life. In our own lives, we may face situations that seem overwhelmimming, but with consistent, sincere prayer, God will move on our behalf. And with just one word, God can change the entire course of our lives.

3. POSSESSION –

Depression eventually connects with the demon of possession, building strongholds that take years to overcome. Possession is Satan's final stage before "wiping out" an individual. Satan organizes his strategy very carefully. Once oppression and depression make a place for possession, its victims lose all self-control, becoming slaves to the possessive force that holds them captive.

Effects of possession can include mental problems, anti-socialism, bodily deformity, muteness, dumbness, deafness, blindness. This is not to say that all persons with these ailments are demon possessed. The Bible tells us of several people whom Jesus healed from sicknesses and conditions, and it never refers to them as being possessed by a spirit, such as in Matthew 15:30:

> *And great multitudes came unto him, having with them those that were lame, blind, dumb, maimed, and many others, and cast them down at Jesus' feet; and he healed them:*

Luke, the disciple and physician who traveled with Jesus, always distinguished between demon-possession and sickness.

Conclusion

The enemy uses three vehicles to attack mankind: oppression, depression, and possession. Oppression is a spirit of heaviness that attaches itself to the physical and spiritual being of the one being oppressed. It can also be manifested through sickness and bad habits. Depression is a spirit that causes worry, doubt, and unbelief. Possession is the enslaving force of a demonic spirit in a person's life. The victim loses all self-control and is dominated by that force until deliverance becomes their portion. One can be set free from oppression through godly music, worship, prayer, resistance, and the Word of God. Possession must be dealt with according to the Word of God. Jesus never touched anyone when casting out demons, He simply spoke the Word and commanded them to leave. We have this same power and ability to speak the Word and command demons to flee, but we must add the name of Jesus to invoke the power that will set the captives free.

****

LESSON REVIEW

1. Name three ways that demons attack mankind.

2. Oppression is like a _____. It carries with it a spirit of _____ that _____ the mind and _____ the thinking.

3. Oppression may be manifested in:
   a) _____
   b) _____

4. List four names of oppression.

5. What Old Testament king was under a heavy spirit of oppression, sent from the Lord?

6. What Old Testament king was oppressed and depressed, and why?

Scripture References:

1 Peter 5:8
Isaiah 14:12-16, 24, 26-27; 38:1-5,14
John 10:10
1 Samuel 18:10-12

The Day I Got Set Free
My Diary of Deliverance

The weapons of our warfare are not carnal, but mighty through God to the pulling down of strongholds. (1 Cor. 10:4)

Date: _____

- ☐ Monday
- ☐ Tuesday
- ☐ Wednesday
- ☐ Thursday
- ☐ Friday
- ☐ Saturday
- ☐ Sunday

**If two of you shall agree on earth as touching any thing that they shall ask, it shall be done for them. (Matthew 18:19)

Today Lord I set myself in agreement with Bishop George Bloomer and the mighty prayer warriors of Bethel Family Worship Center that this yoke will be destroyed in my life, in Jesus' name. Amen

_____

_____

_____

_____

_____

LESSON 7: Oppression, Depression, Possession

_____

_____

_____

_____

_____

_____

_____

_____

_____

_____

_____

_____

_____

_____

_____

_____

_____

_____

_____

_____

LESSON

HOW TO CAST OUT DEMONS

[20]Not withstanding in this rejoice not, that the spirits are subject unto you; but rather rejoice, because your names are written in heaven.

—Luke 10:20

INTRODUCTION

There would be no reason to teach or instruct about demons and spiritual warfare if we knew how to detect and cast them out. In Luke 10:19-20, after Jesus had appointed the seventy, He began to instruct them concerning the authority that they had been given to do the work of the Lord. Every believer who wants to do something for God must be trained by someone who has already engaged in spiritual warfare. In the teachings of Jesus, He always used applications that people were familiar with, so that they could understand what He meant.

Prayer

Lord Jesus,

We thank You for the power that You have granted us, through the Holy Spirit, to tread upon serpents and scorpions, to cast out demons and evil imaginations. May we learn how to follow Your lead and not the steps of man. Teach us; give us revelation; and protect us as we study this aspect of Your Word. Amen.

LESSON

Possession: domination by an evil spirit; a psychological state in which an individual's normal personality is replaced by another

COMMON BARRIERS TO ENGAGING IN SPIRITUAL WARFARE

1. **No faith** – We've all been given a measure of faith, but it's up to us to exercise
   that faith.
2. **No power** – One must first have power before attempting to exercise power to free someone else.
3. **Fear** – Faith combats fear.
4. **Pride** – One must live a life submitted to God in prayer, not seek to receive God's glory, and do all things *only* within His timing.
5. **Religious Spirits and Traditions** – Too many myths concerning deliverance and warfare prevent us from truly engaging in spiritual warfare.

LUKE 10:19-20

DISSECTING AND RIGHTLY DIVIDING THE WORD OF TRUTH

PURPOSE: God's Purpose is not to simply deliver believers from their sins and bring them out of bondage, but to teach them how to properly engage in spiritual warfare.

The power given to the believer is under the direction and control of God. Let's shed some light on the believer's authority in spiritual warfare.

Because God is omnipotent (all-powerful, almighty), He alone has the ability to stop every demonic attack before it happens. When Jesus instructed the seventy, He told them that they needed to become familiar with using that which had been given unto them.

♦ *Behold, I give unto you power...*

Power is the delegated authority, which is given to the believer at the time of salvation.

Satan has always attempted to hinder God's work but delegated power, given to the believer through Jesus Christ, is

far more powerful than the class of
Satan's demons.

♦ *To tread on serpents...*

Represents God's ability to protect us
from the poisonous temptations or
deceptions that Satan uses to injure
his victims. God's promise is to protect
us from danger if we use His spoken
Word at the time of Satan's attack.

Matthew 4:4...When Jesus was
tempted of Satan in the wilderness, He
responded quickly by answering with
the words: It *is written, Man shall not
live by bread alone, but by every word
that proceedeth out of the mouth of
God.*

And in Hebrews 4:12...The swiftness
of God's Word is emphasized.

*For the Word of God is quick and
powerful, and sharper than any two-
edged sword.*

♦ *And scorpions...*

Represents the ability, which God has
given to protect those who are His from
the deception of Satan. A scorpion
has the ability to roll up, and because

his body is white, it appears to be an egg. In Luke 11:12, Jesus presents a clear description of the appearance of the scorpion: *If a son shall ask an egg, will he offer him a scorpion?*

♦ *The enemy...*

Satan, is powerful, but he is not omnipotent—all-powerful. God, in His Divine power, has the ability to preserve believers from the power of Satan. He has control over Satan and his demons.

1 John 3:8: *For this purpose the Son of God was manifested, that he might destroy the works of the devil.*

When Jesus cast out demons, it was always by the Spirit of God. Matthew 12:28: But *if I cast out devils by the Spirit of God, then the kingdom of God is come unto you.*

The Spirit of God represents the power of God. In order to exert power over the enemy, we must be filled with the Holy Spirit of God.

Serpents and scorpions are a prophetic representation of Satan and his demonic host. It was the serpent who tempted Adam and Eve in Genesis Chapter Three, and Jesus, in His teaching, makes the symbolism complete. Both the serpent and scorpion represent the most dangerous forces of spiritual evil.

A STORY OF POSSESSION

1.

¹⁴And when he came to his disciples, he saw a great multitude about them, and the scribes questioning with them. ¹⁵And straightway all the people, when they beheld him, were greatly amazed, and running to him saluted him. ¹⁶And he asked the scribes, What question ye with them?

—Mark 9:14-16

Notice that although the "crowd" seems to be very excited about seeing Jesus, and are even awed by Him, Jesus still remains very focused. Some of us will never be able to war against demons all because of one word: PRIDE! Pride comes before the fall (see Proverbs 16:18)); it's another one of Satan's tactics for keeping you bound and keeping your attention on yourself and away from the Father. But Jesus gets right to the point, "Why are you scribes questioning the disciples?"

2.

> *17And one of the multitude answered and said, Master, I have brought unto thee my son, which hath a dumb spirit; 18And wheresoever he taketh he him, he teareth him: and he foameth, and gnasheth with his teeth, and pineth away: and I spake to thy disciples that they should cast him out; and they could not.*
>
> —Mark 9:17,18

The crowd assumed that because the disciples traveled with Jesus, that they would, of course, have the same power that Jesus possessed. In other words, if Jesus has the power to cast out demons, then surely His disciples – His students – have the power as well. This is where disappointment and unbelief of the multitude began and their reason for questioning the disciples. Had Jesus not shown up, this would have been the perfect opportunity for the scribes to discredit the ministry of Jesus and sow discord in the hearts of the multitude. So Jesus rebuked the disciples for their lack of faith. Surely it would have been the disciples, those who have traveled with Him and personally witnessed His ministry in action, who could have at least possessed enough authority and faith to cast this demon out. This, however, was not the case.

3.

> [19]*He answereth him, and saith, O faithless generation, how long shall I be with you? how long shall I suffer you? bring him unto me.*

Jesus does not begin addressing the disciples yet, but essentially the message of the text is relayed to the father of the possessed young man; and the message is simply this:

> "You could cure your son if only you had enough faith to do so; and stop leaning on the arms of other intercessors, building your life and leaning on the arms of others, but instead begin to partner with God."

4.

> [20]*And they brought him unto him: and when he saw him, straightway the spirit tare him; and he fell on the ground, and wallowed foaming.*
> —Mark 9:19,20

Demons recognize the power of God!

5.

> [21]*And he asked his father, How long is it ago since this came unto him? And he said, Of a child.*
> [22]*And ofttimes it hath cast him into the fire, and into the waters, to destroy*

him: but if thou canst do any thing, have compassion on us, and help us.
—Mark 9:21,22

This gives us the history of this demon. He had resided within the young man for quite some time, and was in no way ready to just give up his comfortable abode, especially to a group of individuals who were not operating in faith.

6.

[23]Jesus said unto him, If thou canst believe, all things are possible to him that believeth.
[24]And straightway the father of the child cried out, and said with tears, Lord, I believe; help thou mine unbelief.
—Mark 9:23,24

Although the father is praying to God to help his unbelief as it relates to the healing and deliverance of his son, he already has faith in God to increase his faith. Normally, you only ask from those whom you have faith in to deliver your request.

7.

[25]When Jesus saw that the people came running together...

Notice, Jesus did not rebuke the spirit until the crowd gathered.

> *...he rebuked the foul spirit, saying unto him, Thou dumb and deaf spirit, I charge thee, come out of him, and enter no more into him.*
>
> —Mark 9:25

Again, Jesus wastes no time, but exercises His power and authority by simply commanding the spirit to **come out. He rebukes the spirit.** This was an oppressive spirit, and oppressive spirits must be rebuked. The word "rebuke" is often a word taken out of context, which many mistakenly translate as having a person rolling around on the floor, laying hands on them, and making a scene. On the contrary, however, "rebuke" means simply to reprimand sharply, to correct. So Jesus took authority over the spirit and it departed from him.

8.

> *²⁶And the spirit cried, and rent him sore, and came out of him: and he was as one dead; insomuch that many said, He is dead.*
>
> —Mark 9:26

Notice that upon exiting the young man's body, the spirit "rent" him. The spirit knew at the spoken Word of Jesus that he had to come out. But his purpose was to kill the man's son in the process. This is why timing is always important when casting out demons. You should never endanger the life of an individual by playing spiritual games, or doing things outside of the will and timing of God. If done within God's will and timing, however, no matter how hard the demonic force fights to remain inside the body, he has to come out, and the hand of God will protect the individual's life during the process of this demonic exodus.

9.

[27] But Jesus took him by the hand, and lifted him up; and he arose.
[28] And when he was come into the house, his disciples asked him privately, Why could not we cast him out?
[29] And he said unto them, This kind can come forth by nothing, but by prayer and fasting.
—Mark 9:27-29

Essentially what Jesus was saying to the disciples was, "Had you been praying and fasting as you should have, you would have had enough faith and power to cast this demon out." The disciples should have been living a lifestyle of prayer and fasting, submit- ting themselves to the perfect will of God.

In Matthew 17:20, Jesus reminds the disciples that you don't need a whole lot of faith to deal with oppressive demons. Likewise, we're to be mindful of this very important fact:

> *...If ye have faith as a grain of a mustard seed, ye shall say unto this mountain, Remove hence to yonder place; and it shall remove; and nothing shall be impossible unto you.*
> —Matthew 17:20b

Jesus does not even demand that we have faith as an entire mustard seed, but simply a "grain" of mustard seed. Mustard seeds come in clusters. When you pull back the leaves, there are several grains, each about the size of a grain of salt. And if you have just that amount of faith, that's all it takes to impel even the demonic mountains of oppression.

Leaders oftentimes make the mistake of waiting until they're confronted with issues before they pray or fast, thus yielding no results. If one is to take on the task of casting out demons, or engaging in spiritual warfare, he or she must live a lifestyle submitted to God, have a relationship established with God, and have a name that's known in the principalities of darkness.

We all remember the popular story of the seven sons of Skeva (Acts 19:13-18). "Paul I know, Jesus I know, but who are you?" (Acts 19:15). If we're not careful, this too will become our testimony if we attempt to come against Satan's kingdom through fleshly means.

SPEAK THE WORD ONLY!

Another trick of the enemy is to hinder us through religious and traditional doctrines to the point that constant exposure to the Word of God has little or no effect. Consequently, we wander in circles, wrestling with demons, screaming, making a scene, because we no longer have enough faith in the simplicity of the Word of God. We begin to feel that God somehow needs our help in fighting evil forces, thus acquiescing to the subtle deception and temptation of Lucifer to fight him through man-made tactics. Lucifer knows the Word. He also knows that he can only be defeated by the Word. His strategy, then, becomes to dissuade us from following Jesus' example—speaking the Word.

Conclusion

The kingdom of darkness will try to hinder us through religious and traditional doctrines. Pride comes before a fall, and keeps you focused on yourself, rather than on the Father. Demons recognize the power of God. Demons will not exit a body if those praying for the victim have no faith. All we need to do is to have faith the size of a mustard seed, and even demonic "mountains" will have to move. Jesus did not go through an entire ritual; instead, He simply commanded the demon to come out and it was done. Upon exiting a body, demons will try to kill the victim. This is why the timing of God is imperative; for the hand of God will protect the individual in the midst of this process. We must live a lifestyle dedicated to fasting and prayer so that we will be ready in season and out of season for the Master's work. At the word of Jesus, the spirit came out of the young man. We can also command demons to flee in our own lives, and in the lives of others by using the name of Jesus. If we have faith in His Word, even the size of a grain of a mustard seed, the power of that faith in Jesus' name gives demons no choice but to flee!

****

LESSON REVIEW

1. Name two barriers to engaging in spiritual warfare.

2. What is power?

3. What can a scorpion be mistaken for? What is the importance of that metaphor?

4. What do the serpent and the scorpion represent in scripture?

5. Demons recognize the _____ of _____.

6. What example of Jesus can we follow in order to defeat the enemy?

Scripture References:

Luke 10:19-20; 11:12
Matthew 4:4, 12:28; 17:20
1 John 3:8
Genesis 3
Mark 9:14-29
Acts 19:13-18

The Day I Got Set Free

My Diary of Deliverance

The weapons of our warfare are not carnal, but mighty through God to the pulling down of strongholds. (1 Cor. 10:4)

Date: _____

- ☐ Monday
- ☐ Tuesday
- ☐ Wednesday
- ☐ Thursday
- ☐ Friday
- ☐ Saturday
- ☐ Sunday

***If two of you shall agree on earth as touching any thing that they shall ask, it shall be done for them. (Matthew 18:19)**

Today Lord I set myself in agreement with Bishop George Bloomer and the mighty prayer warriors of Bethel Family Worship Center that this yoke will be destroyed in my life, in Jesus' name. Amen

_____

_____

_____

_____

_____

LESSON 8: How To Cast Out Demons

_____

_____

_____

_____

_____

_____

_____

_____

_____

_____

_____

_____

_____

_____

_____

_____

_____

_____

_____

_____

_____

_____

_____

LESSON

PHASES OF DEMONOLOGY

[20]But I say, that the things which the Gentiles sacrifice, they sacrifice to devils and not to God: and I would not that ye should have fellowship with devils.   —1 Corinthians 10:20

INTRODUCTION

God was bringing His people into a land populated with people who worked all kinds of abominations before the God of heaven. He did not want Israel to become contaminated with these things, so he instructed them not to take an interest in, learn, nor participate in these vile acts.

Prayer

Lord Jesus,

Thank You for the truths of Your Word, and for bringing to light, all the hidden things of the darkness. Amen.

LESSON

WHAT IS DEMONOLOGY?

Demonology - the study of demons, a treatise on demons or demon worship, or a belief in demons.

The Three Pillars of Demonology

Three words describe the occult:

♦ *Divination* - the fortune-telling realm of the spirit
♦ *Sorcery* - the use of power gained from the assistance/control of evil spirits
♦ *Witchcraft* - the dominating realm of the spirit

Let's take a look at these facets of demonology:

1. DIVINATION
   The act or art of foretelling the unknown; sometimes by use of the stars or evil spirits. Has been referred to as the counterfeit of Bible prophecy. There are several branches of divination. Each branch seeks to acquire concealed information of past, present, and future events by supernatural means. Several methods are used in divination in an effort to make contact with evil spirits and/or control them; and also to foretell the future. These methods include clairvoyance, mediums, stars, enchantments, trances, and dreams.

   *Works Through: tarot cards, tea leaves, crystal balls, horoscopes, palm reading, trances, dreams, enchantments.

   *Bible References: *Genesis 44:5,15; Deuteronomy 18:10-14, 2 Kings 17:17, 21:6; *Ezekiel 21:21-23; *22:28;

Acts 16:16

*In Genesis 44:5,15, a divining cup is mentioned. Diviners would put water and oil in a cup and then interpret the shape of the oil floating on top of the water.

*In Ezekiel 21:21-23, diviners would read and interpret the livers of sacrificial animals to foretell the future. It also mentions the use of making arrows bright. They would throw down a handful of arrows, hoping that a certain one would point to a route that they believed was the will of the gods.

*In Ezekiel 22:28, the prophets would deceive people, telling them that there was a word from the Lord; but they were telling lies in the name of God.

2. SORCERY
   The utilization of power attained from the assistance or control of evil spirits. Derived from the Greek word *pharmakia*, which means *pharmacy* in the English language. This definitely has an association with drugs, and applies to mind-altering sub-stances or those who use drugs to bring on trances, during which they may claim to have supernatural power.

*Works Through: drugs, alcohol, suggestive dancing, charms, and the ancient wearing of make-up

*Bible References: Acts 8:9-25, 13:6-8; Revelation 9:21, 18:23, 21:8, 22:15, Exodus 7:11, Jeremiah 27:9, Isaiah 57:3

3. <u>WITCHCRAFT</u>
The art or skill of using supernatural forces to bend the world to one's will. It involves divination or sorcery that attempted to avoid or alter God's revealed will, as in the story of the witch of Endor in 1 Samuel 28.

*Works Through: disobedience (this opens the door to intimidation, manipulation and domination–to be mentioned in more detail later in this chapter)

*Bible References: Deuteronomy 18:9-14; Jeremiah 27:8-11, 29:8,9; Nahum 3:1-4; 1 Samuel 28:7-20, 1 Chronicles 10:13

DEMONOLOGY IN THE OLD TESTAMENT

The nation of Israel had been in contact with surrounding nations who worshipped other dieties—idols. They practiced ungodly rituals, and were deep into spiritism. So God commanded them not to be influenced by their neighbors in the following passage:

There shall not be found among you any one that **maketh his son or his daughter to pass through the fire**, *or that useth* **divination**, *or an* **observer of times**, *or an* **enchanter**, *or a* **witch**, *Or a* **charmer**, *or* **consulter with familiar spirits**, *or a* **wizard**, *or a* **necromancer**. *For all that do these things are an abomination unto to Lord: and because these are abominations the Lord thy God doth drive them out from before thee.*

—Deuteronomy 18:10-12

Let us get a better understanding of exactly what was occurring at the time of this command:

1. **Making his son or his daughter to pass through the fire**
2. **Divination**
3. **Observer of times (Astrology)**
4. **Witch**
5. **Enchanter**
6. **Charmer**
7. **Consulters of familiar spirits**
8. **Wizard**
9. **Necromancer**

1. HUMAN SACRIFICE BY FIRE

The practice of offering up a person, usually a child upon an altar engulfed with fire, to appease the gods (demons) and receive demonic power and favor from them.

This method of child sacrifice was done to appease the god Molech (2 Kings 23:10), the gods Adrammelech and Anammelech - the gods of Sepharvaim (2 Kings 17:31) and, of course, the god Baal (Jeremiah 19:5). Wicked King Manasseh sacrificed his children in this manner (2 Kings 21:6; 2 Chronicles 33:6). Also his grandfather, King Ahaz, burnt his children two generations earlier in 2 Kings 16:3 and 2 Chronicles 28:3.

This is in complete contradiction to the Word of God. The sacrifices that God required of the children of Israel were for the atonement of sin, not to appease God or receive power from Him. God also gave instructions in the book of Leviticus regarding the offerings that He would receive from His people. John 3:16 says, *For God so loved the world, that he gave his only begotten Son, that whosoever believeth in him should not perish, but have everlasting life.* The Father loved us so much that He gave what was most valuable to Him in order to reconcile us back to Himself. It is not God's design that we sacrifice human life. This is perversion from the enemy.

2. DIVINATION

Previously discussed, however, we will attempt to break it down into more detail. Divination is the art or act of foretelling future events or acquiring occultic knowledge through the means of augury (a sign or omen; indication) or alleged supernatural agency. An inspired guess or a presentiment.

Common forms of this Practice:

- ◆ Palm-reading
- ◆ Crystal ball-reading
- ◆ Water-witching**
- ◆ Pendulum
- ◆ Divining
- ◆ Tarot card-reading
- ◆ Tea leaf-reading
- ◆ Numerology
- ◆ Study of Animal entrails.

*** The practice of finding water underground by means of a divining or rod or the likes.*

As society becomes more scientifically and technologically advanced, Satan has also come along to contaminate various techniques, which would normally offer godly, legitimate information, and he instead has employed demons to expand their range to give large sums of information. Three examples of this would be: Iridology, Graph analysis and Hypnosis. Let's take a look at these:

Iridology: The practice that makes the claim that by looking into the iris (colored portion) of the eye, any disorder or sickness can be diagnosed.

Graph analysis: Also called handwriting analysis. This method is all right for determining whether a signature is a forgery, or whether a person is a male or female for investigative purposes, but it becomes something other than natural when someone begins to tell you things about past events in your life. This is divination.

Hypnosis: An artificially-induced, sleeplike condition in which an individual is extremely responsive to suggestions made by the hypnotist. To allow oneself to be hypnotized is in violation of the Word of God, and gives Satan legal ground to afflict and torment the person under hypnosis. Hypnosis is nothing more than a demonic trance. God has instructed us to guard our minds.

I Peter 1:13:
Wherefore gird up the lions of your mind, be sober, and hope to the end for the grace that is to be brought unto you at the revelation of Jesus Christ.

II Corinthians 10:3-5:
³For though we walk in the flesh, we do not war after the flesh:

[4](For the weapons of our warfare are not carnal, but mighty through God to the pulling down of strong holds;)
[5]Casting down imaginations, and every high thing that exalteth itself against the knowledge of God, and bringing into captivity every thought to the obedience of Christ;

I Peter 5:8:
Be sober be, be vigilant; because your adversary the devil, as a roaring lion, walketh about, seeking whom he may devour:

If the Word of God admonishes us to gird up the lions of our mind, to be sober and watchful, and to cast down imaginations and every thing that exalts itself against the Word of God, how can we possibly allow ourselves to be hypnotized, or falsely slain in the spirit? I bring up this topic not because I do not believe in being slain in the spirit. I believe that it is very real; however, many people that I have encountered say that when they have been slain, they have blanked out completely. Yet others say that when they have been slain, they have received instruction from God, saw a vision, or heard scripture. From early passages, and the scripture above, we know that the Holy Spirit desires our cooperation, and that God expects us to be alert to what's going on. So we must be careful when allowing just anyone to lay their hands upon us.

3. OBSERVER OF TIMES

Observer of times is a synonym often used for a *sorcerer*. The observer of times is one who casts spells, and attempts to control people or circumstances through power given by an evil spirit, or a demon. Also known for using herbs, charts, and a myriad of potions.

4. WITCH

One who is involved in the practice of magical incantation.

5. ENCHANTER

Also known as an *astrologer* or a *conjurer*. The word *conjurer* denotes *to whisper, to blow, or to breathe*. He is one who interprets omens, or tells the future based on signs of fire, rain, or the movement of birds. Could be considered a palm reader, a fortune-teller, an astrologer, who claims to be able to tell the future by seeing the movement of the stars.

6. CHARMER

One who casts spells, or one who ties knots, who bind people with magic mutterings.

7. CONSULTER OF FAMILIAR SPIRITS

One who is a medium (a person thought to have power to communicate with the dead) or a séance leader—a necromancer. He seeks to communicate with the dead, but communicates with demons.

8. WIZARD

One who participates in the art or practice of witchcraft and sorcery.

9. NECROMANCER

One who interrogates the dead, a medium or a spiritist, a consulter of spirits.

WHY IS OUR GOD SO AGAINST THE ENTERTAINING OF THESE PRACTICES?

It is because they are:
◆ **Deadly**

Thou shalt not suffer a witch to live.
　　　　　　　　—Exodus 22:18

26And ye shall be holy unto me: for I the Lord am holy, and have severed you from other people, that ye should be mine.

27A man also or woman that hath a familiar spirit, or that is a wizard, shall surely be put to death: they shall stone them with stones: their blood shall be upon them.
—Leviticus 20:26,27

♦ **Demonically Orchestrated**

13So Saul died for his transgression which he committed against the LORD, even against the word of the LORD, which he kept not, and also for asking counsel of one that had a familiar spirit, to enquire of it;
14And enquired not of the LORD: therefore he slew him, and turned the kingdom unto David the son of Jesse.

—I Chronicles 10:13,14

♦ **Defiling**

Regard not them that have familiar spirits, neither seek after wizards, to be defiled by them: I am the LORD your God.
—Leviticus 19:31

And he caused his children to pass through the fire in the valley of the son of Hinnom: also he observed times, and used enchantments, and used witchcraft, and dealt with a familiar spirit, and with wizards: he wrought much evil in the sight of the LORD, to provoke Him to anger.

—II Chronicles 33:6

♦ **Dark Forces**

[19]And when they shall say unto you, Seek unto them that have familiar spirits, and unto wizards that peep, and that mutter: should not a people seek unto their God? for the living to the dead?
[20]To the law and to the testimony: if they speak not according to this word, it is because there is no light in them.

—Isaiah 8: 19,20 (see also verses 21-22)

♦ **Deceiving**
And the light of a candle shall shine no more at all in thee; and the voice of the bridegroom and of the bride shall be heard no more at all in thee: for thy merchants were the great men of the earth; for by thy sorceries were all nations deceived.
—Revelations 18:23

♦ **Damning**

> *But the fearful, and unbelieving, and
> the abominable, and murderers, and
> whoremongers, and sorcerers, and
> idolaters, and all liars, shall have their
> part in the lake which burneth with fire
> and brimstone: which is the second
> death.*
> —Revelations 21:8

> *For without are dogs, and sorcerers,
> and whoremongers, and murderers,
> and idolaters, and whosoever loveth
> and maketh a lie.*
> —Revelations 22:15

Our Father, in His great wisdom, knows the outcome of these arts and practices. We, again, would do well to heed His instruction.

Conclusion

The three pillars of demonology are: divination, sorcery, and witchcraft. Divination is the fortune-telling realm of the spirit; sorcery is the use of power gained from the assistance or control of evil spirits, and witchcraft is the dominating realm of the spirit. *Divination* includes a wide variety of occultic methods; some of which include: hypnosis, graph analysis, and iridology. *Sorcery* involves using drugs, both the pharmaceutical and illegal kind. The drugs give a high, placing one in a trance and captivating him or her, both in mind and body. Their victim feels good physically and his or her desire is to get as much of the drug as possible in order to maintain that feeling. This is what has so captivated our young people in today's world of drug phenomenon and paraphernalia. Drugs are controlling and entrancing. Finally, *witchcraft* is another huge branch of demonology. It includes mysticism, soothsaying, and telepathy, which we will discuss in further detail in the next lesson.

One can break free from these chains of darkness by confessing the Word aloud and denouncing Satan and his forces. Once you've done this, you do not have to wait for a certain feeling; just believe the Word of God — that God has forgiven you and set you free indeed. You can then move in step with the Holy Spirit.

****

LESSON REVIEW

1. What are the three pillars of demonology?

2. From what Greek word is the word *sorcery* derived? What does this Greek word suggest?

3. What royal grandfather and grandson practiced child sacrifice?

4. Why is God against demonology? Give six reasons.

5. What is another synonym for sorcerer as described in this lesson?

6. Name the practice, which is used by psychiatrists even today, that causes one to fall into a trance. From what pillar of demonology is this practice derived?

Scripture References:

1 Corinthians 10:20-21
Genesis 44:5, 15
Deuteronomy 18:10-14
2 Kings 17:17,31; 21:6; 23:10; 16:3

The Day I Got Set Free

My Diary of Deliverance

The weapons of our warfare are not carnal, but mighty through God to the pulling down of strongholds. (1 Cor. 10:4)

Date: _____

- ☐ Monday
- ☐ Tuesday
- ☐ Wednesday
- ☐ Thursday
- ☐ Friday
- ☐ Saturday
- ☐ Sunday

***If two of you shall agree on earth as touching any thing that they shall ask, it shall be done for them. (Matthew 18:19)**

Today Lord I set myself in agreement with Bishop George Bloomer and the mighty prayer warriors of Bethel Family Worship Center that this yoke will be destroyed in my life, in Jesus' name. Amen

_____

_____

_____

_____

LESSON 9: Phases of Demonology

Personal Notes:

_____

_____

_____

_____

_____

_____

_____

_____

_____

_____

_____

_____

_____

_____

_____

_____

_____

_____

_____

LESSON 9: Phases of Demonology

_____

_____

_____

_____

_____

_____

_____

_____

_____

_____

_____

_____

_____

_____

_____

_____

_____

_____

_____

_____

LESSON

WHAT IS WITCHCRAFT?

For false christs and false prophets shall rise, and shall show signs and wonders, to seduce, if it were possible, even the elect. But take ye heed: behold, I have foretold you all things.   —Mark 13:22-23

INTRODUCTION

The Word of God says that Satan is a deceiver (Revelation 12:9). He will go to any means necessary to distract and eventually convince an individual of his lies (John 8:44). He uses subtleties from the media and even the church itself for his work. There are different forms of witchcraft, which you will soon discover in this lesson.

Prayer

Lord Jesus,

Thank You for revealing to us the darkness of Lucifer's kingdom and his subtle entrapments. Now equip us to tear his kingdom down for Your glory. Amen.

LESSON

IT'S ORIGIN: THE TOWER OF BABEL

Witchcraft: The art of turning another person's will to your will.

All forms of witchcraft, including magic and mysticism, derive from the Tower of Babel (Genesis 11:1-9). This infamous tower was built not long after Noah's flood, in what we refer to today as the modern nation of Iraq. It is important that we understand the Tower of Babel and its purpose, because it is the birth-place of witchcraft. It was built for two main reasons:

1. to worship idol gods
2. to study the host of heaven (stars, moon, and planets, from whence comes astrology).

The word *witch* is derived form the Indo-European root word, *weik*, which means *religion* and *magic*. The word *witchcraft* comes from an old English term *wicce-craft,* which refers to *the art or skill of using supernatural forces to bend the world to one's will.*

So witchcraft is a religion that worships Satan and his demonic forces in order to receive magic power to influence the wills of others. In modern-day society, it is sometimes referred to as the religion of Wicca.

SOME FORMS OF WITCHCRAFT

A.   NECROMANCY

Communication with the dead. This refers to seances. An account of an actual séance in the Bible is found in 1 Samuel 28:7-20. Israel's first king, Saul, sought out a witch to call up the spirit of the dead prophet Samuel. An apparition appeared before him and spoke with him (There is argument about whether or not it was really the spirit of Samuel or a demonic impersonation).

*Works Through: seances, ventriloquism

*Bible References: Deuteronomy18:10-12, *Isaiah 8:19

*Isaiah 8:19 refers to wizards who *peep and mutter*—those who cause the voice to seem to come from lower regions, thus inferring ventriloquism.

B. <u>SOOTHSAYING</u>
The act of foretelling events. The Hebrew word for *soothsaying* *(*anan*) sounds like the Hebrew word for *cloud* *(*anan*). Some believe that it refers to cloud reading. It may be linked to tea leaf reading or astrology.

*Works Through: weather, omens, horoscopes, astrology, crystal gazing, fortune-telling, palmistry, tarot cards

*Bible References: Isaiah 2:6, Micah 5:12

* In the Hebrew language, there are four words that are spelt a-n-a-n. They each have slightly different sounds. (See Strong's 6049-6052).

C. TELEPATHY

Communication from one mind to another by extrasensory means: mind-reading and/or thought-sending. Those who participate in this activity are acquiescing their minds and spirits to the forces of Satan. The only mind-reader should be God.
(Psalms 139:2)

*Works Through: hypnosis, E.S.P., subliminal messages

*Bible References: *Daniel 2

*In Daniel 2, King Nebuchadnezzar desired that sorcerers, astrologers, etc. would tell him what he dreamed.

D. MYSTICISM

The doctrine that knowledge of reality, God, truth, etc. is attainable by direct revelation, intuition, or spiritual insight, without the medium of the senses or reason.

The scribes and the Pharisees were a prime example of this doctrine. They sought signs but were not interested in seeking a relationship with God.

*Works Through: thrill-seeking, melodrama, feelings, theatrics

*Bible References: Matthew 12:38-39

E. ASTROLOGY
The dividing of the heavens for the purpose of prophecy and divination, or to make a horoscope. Astrology professes to discover certain connections between the positions and movements of the planets and events, which occur in the earth. Practiced in ancient times through observing the rising and setting of the planets, their orbits and their color (could predict storms, heat, rain, comets, eclipses, earthquakes and ordinary human affairs). Stars and planets were divided into what they called *houses*. The positions of the stars within the houses determined their calculations. God created the stars for signs, seasons, days, and years (Genesis 1:14), not to be worshipped. He also created them to give light in the heavens as well as upon the earth (Genesis 1:15). The heavens were created to declare the glory of the Living God (Psalm 19:1).

*Works Through: stars and stargazing, planets, horoscopes

*Bible References: Isaiah 47:13, Daniel 1:20; 2:2,10, 27; 4:7; 5:7, 11, 15

F. INTERPRETING OMENS
The act of interpreting an occurrence or phenomenon believed to portend a future event. Four different Hebrew words describe this phrase. The one that is most often used, *nachash*, can be found in Genesis 30:27, which tells of Laban's *experience:*

> And Laban said unto him...for I have learned by **experience** that the Lord hath blessed me...

It can also be found in Genesis 44:5, 15 in reference to Joseph's cup, and also in Numbers 23:23 and 24:1 in reference to the actions of Balaam. This phrase is interpretied as *enchantments.* One of the other Hebrew words seems to indicate whispering, implying that voices were lowered during enchantments. Augurs (those who interpreted omens) would also foretell the future by observing the flight of birds. Snake charming has also been associated with omens, as seen in Ecclesiastes 10:11.

*Works Through: signs (e.g. weather, incidents, and so on), bird watching

*Bible References: *Matthew 16:1-3

*The Pharisees and Saducees studied the weather for signs of things to come.

G. CONJURING SPELLS
   The contrivance of spoken words or formulas designed to produce a particular effect. Also referred to as *charm* (used in scriptures referenced below). Also translated as *enchantments* (from another Hebrew word), as it is associated with the word *bind*, suggesting spellbinding or casting a spell.

   Works Through: magic, incantations, charms, jugglers, enchantments, conjuration.

   Bible Reference: Deuteronomy 18:10-11; Psalms 58:5; Isaiah 47:9,12.

LEGEND OR REALITY

Some of you may wonder if these are just legendary tales and/or myths. You are probably thinking to yourself, "If I haven't seen it, I just don't believe it." But I cannot emphasize enough that this is real. As explained in the Lesson Four, Lucifer and his forces have real powers and are very active in today's world. They have the power to perform signs and the power to deceive. However, just remember, he can only do what God permits him to do. Therefore, he is limited.

Others of you may think that witchcraft is no longer active in today's world. You don't see witches trafficking the skies on broomsticks, so these lessons are just absurd to you. But witchcraft is taking place in today's modern world. It is quite subtle these days in the form of movies, video games, board games, toys, music, psychic hotlines, new religions, yoga, tarot cards, horoscopes, palm reading, fortune telling, magic tricks, and of course, **Halloween**, just to name a few.

WHY CHRISTIANS SHOULDN'T CELEBRATE HALLOWEEN

1. In what country did Halloween originate, and how did it find its way to America?

Halloween was introduced to this country during the mid-1800's. When thousands of Catholic Irish immigrants, fleeing the potato famine in Ireland, came to the United States. Since that time, Halloween has become a custom and a cultural celebration in most American homes, schools, and churches. It is observed by children going door to door asking for and receiving candy (called treats); and if their request is not honored, threats to commit pranks are made (called tricks). Others celebrate with masked and costume parties, haunted houses, horror movies, and the like. Black cats, jack-o-lanterns (pumpkins), witches, ghosts, TV characters, and monsters have all become a part of the celebrations.

2. Is Halloween recognized by the U.S. Government?

At first, Halloween was discouraged because of its pagan roots, but its celebrations have still persisted. Despite these celebrations, however, the United States government still does not recognize Halloween as an official holiday in this country. Nonetheless, the IRS has granted tax exemption to the Church of Wicca (old word for *witch*), one of Halloween's biggest participants, thereby legalizing and recognizing witchcraft as a religion.

3. What is the history behind Halloween?

The earliest celebrations originated with the Celts before the birth of Christ. The Celts were a pagan people who worshipped many gods. The Celtic Druids observed October 31st as their New Year's Eve with the Festival of Samhain. This was the celebration and worship of the dead. They believed that on the evening of October 31st, the spirits of the dead revisited their earthly homes. The soul of the departed was transferred by magic to the body of an animal.

Also on this night, Samhain, lord of the dead, called forth hosts of evil spirits. Huge fires were set on hilltops to frighten the evil spirits and consume the people's sacrifices. They sacrificed their animals, and sometimes humans, in an attempt to appease their gods. As personal protection from the spirit world, the people wore disguises made of animal heads and skins. This is the beginning of the masks and costumes worn on Halloween.

Food treats were provided for the evil spirits to prevent them from playing wicked tricks on the people. This is the same tradition today wherein people dress up in costumes, knock on doors, and say, "Trick or Treat." Just as people once offered gifts of food to the spirits, people today offer treats to the children who represent the spirits.

SYMBOLS OF HALLOWEEN

Halloween was the only time of year in which the devil was called upon to help in divination, in regard to people's fate and health for the coming year. The following symbols were a few of the ways the people of this time would communicate with evil spirits for protection and romance:

1. The Jack-O-Lantern

Carved pumpkins symbolize two things:

1. Witches would use a skull with a candle in it to light the way to coven meetings

2. Druids would use large turnips carved with demonic faces, and lit with burning coals. They placed them outside each home as further protection from the evil spirits.

The lighted turnip face, or Jack-o-Lantern, is the ancient symbol for a damned soul. When the Irish brought this holiday to America, pumpkins were substituted for turnips. The lighted Jack-o-Lanterns, which the children carry, are really a symbol of the fires and torches used by the ancient Samhain.

The Legend of the Jack-O-Lantern

There is a legend of a man called "Irish Jack," who was a stingy drunk that tricked the devil into climbing a tree for an apple, but then cut the sign of the cross in the trunk of the tree, which prevented the devil from coming down. Jack made the devil swear he would never come after Jack's soul. The devil agreed. When Jack died, he was turned away from the gates of heaven because of his drunkenness and life of selfishness. He was sent to the devil, who also rejected him because of his promise. Since Jack had nowhere to go, he was condemned to wander the earth. As he was leaving hell, (he happened to be eating a turnip), the devil threw a live coal at him. As the story goes, Jack put the coal inside the turnip and has been roaming on earth with his jack-o-lantern in search of a place of rest.

3. Bobbing for Apples

The Romans had a festival for the dead, which was celebrated in late October. On Nov. 1 they celebrated the goddess of the fruit trees. The Roman and Celtic cultures were combined. Three sacred fruits of the Celtics were acorns, apples, and nuts. That's why bobbing for apples is done on Halloween. Dunking for apples became an aspect of romantic divination for discovering your future mate.

4. Black Cat

The black cat was both reverenced and feared by pagan people. It was believed that black cats were once persons changed into cats as punishment for their sins. This was part of the occult teaching of reincarnation, which also included the teaching that the corpse of Dracula lives at night and can change into a bat during the day.

5. Witches

Halloween is the most important "witches' sabbath," and is referred to as "the devil's holiday." This is an evening when witches and their followers meet to worship the devil. New members are initiated on Halloween, and must take an oath of obedience to the devil, and sign contracts in blood. The sabbath continues with worship, dancing, and ends in a sexual orgy. Genuine witches and their followers still preserve the early pagan beliefs, and consider Halloween the "High, Holy Day" in witchcraft.

INTIMIDATION, MANIPULATION & DOMINATION:

3 Major Components of Witchcraft

A) **Intimidation** says, "I will scare you into doing what I want".

*[16]Saying, What shall we do to these men? for that indeed a notable miracle hath been done by them is manifest to all them that dwell in Jerusalem; and we cannot deny it.
[17]But that it spread no further among the people, let us straitly threaten them, that they speak henceforth to no man in his name.
[18]And they called them, and commanded them not to speak at all nor teach in the name of Jesus.
[19]But Peter and John answered and said unto them, Whether it be right in the sight of God to hearken unto you more than unto God, judge ye.*

[20]For we cannot but speak the things which we have seen and heard.

—Acts 4:16-20

The rulers sought to cease the works of God by hindering the ministry of Peter and John through intimidation. The rulers admit that there is no way for them to deny the miracle that was performed, so they were forced to devise a plan to prevent the Word from spreading by threatening and intimidating them (verse 17).

When you know who you are in Christ, however, the boldness of God outweighs any intimidation that man attempts. So Peter and John end by saying, *We can only speak the things which we have seen and heard.*

B) **Manipulation** - says, "I will trick you into doing what I want or giving me what I need."

[4]And it came to pass afterward, that he loved a woman in the valley of Sorek, whose name was Delilah.
[5]And the lords of the Philistines came up unto her, and said unto her, Entice him, and see wherein his great strength lieth, and by what means we may prevail against him, that we bind him to afflict

him: and we will give thee every one of us eleven hundred pieces of silver.
⁶And Delilah said to Samson, Tell me, I pray thee, wherein thy great strength lieth, and wherewith thou mightest be bound to afflict thee.

¹⁵And she said unto him (Samson), How canst thou say, I love thee, when thine heart is not with me? thou hast mocked me these three times, and hast not told me wherein thy great strength lieth.
—Judges 16:4-6,15

So finally, Samson gives into her manipulation.

¹⁶And it came to pass, when she pressed him daily with her words, and urged him, so that his soul was vexed unto death;
¹⁷That he told her all his heart, and said unto her, There hath not come a razor upon mine head; for I have been a Nazarite unto God from my mother's womb: if I be shaven, then my strength will go from me, and I shall become weak, and be like any other man.
—Judges 16:16,17

Because Samson loved Delilah, she was able to manipulate from him his most prized possession—his strength.

The story has a bitter-sweet ending with Samson's death. in his death, he slew more than he did in his life by pulling down the pillars and collapsing the house that was full of Philistines.

C) **Domination**: Says, "I will force you to do what I want."

> *⁴Then an herald cried aloud, To you it is commanded, O people, nations, and languages,*
> *⁵That at what time ye hear the sound of the cornet, flute, harp, sackbut, psaltery, dulcimer, and all kinds of musick, ye fall down and worship the golden image that Nebuchadnezzar the king hath set up:*
> *⁶And whoso falleth not down and worshippeth shall the same hour be cast into the midst of a burning fiery furnace.*
> —Daniel 3:4-6

The king, Nebuchadnezzar, created a new law, which forced everyone to worship the golden image that he created. They had to fall down and worship whenever they heard the orchestra playing aloud. If anyone chose to disobey, he or she would be cast into a fiery furnace. This was clearly a dominating king.

> *¹²There are certain Jews whom thou hast set over the affairs of the province of Babylon, Shadrach, Meshach, and*

Abednego; these men, O king, have not regarded thee: they serve not thy gods, nor worship the golden image which thou hast set up.

—Daniel 3:12

The Chaldeans went to the king and told him that three of his highly esteemed employees did not bow down to the golden image.

19Then was Nebuchadnezzar full of fury, and the form of his visage was changed against Shadrach, Meshach, and Abednego: therefore he spake, and commanded that they should heat the furnace one seven times more than it was wont to be heated.

23And these three men, Shadrach, Meshach, and Abednego, fell down bound into the midst of the burning fiery furnace.

—Daniel 3:19,23

King Nebuchadnezzar was outraged at these allegations. Who would dare defy his orders by refusing to worship the beautiful image that he created? And three of his best paid workers at that! He would force them to do what he wanted, or they would die. Domination will drive a person to the point of murder. Just think of all the domestic disputes, for example, that end up in murder each year on account of "loving" significant others.

So King Nebuchadnezzar called for his employees, and gave them another chance to obey his new decree. But regardless of his orders, his employees chose to serve God only, and to risk losing their lives.

> [24]*Then Nebuchadnezzar the king was astonished, and rose up in haste, and spake, and said unto his counsellors, Did not we cast three men bound Into the midst of the fire? They answered and said unto the king, True, O king.*
> [25]*He answered and said, Lo, I see four men loose, walking in the midst of the fire, and they have no hurt; and the form of the fourth is like the Son of God.*
>
> —Daniel 3:24,25

When the three boys were thrown into the fiery furnace, the king realized that he didn't hear any screams of torment. He rose up, looked further into the furnace, and just to be sure that he wasn't seeing apparitions, he conferred with his counselors, asking them, "Is it just me, or do I see four men in the furnace, instead of three? And they aren't bound, they're loose! And the fourth guy looks like the Son of God!" The counselors responded, " You're not seeing things at all! Yes, king, you're right!"

Conclusion

Witchcraft works through intimidation, manipulation, and domination. It is real and is still taking place in today's modern world. It creates a false dependence upon natural interpretation of the past, present, and future; and ignores the need for God in one's life. We can be forgiven and set free from these sins if we have ever been involved in them. God has given us weapons to fight against the enemy in every way that he chooses to attack us. If we are consistent in keeping on our godly armor, the enemy cannot destroy us through the bondage of strongholds. We have victory through our Lord Jesus Christ. The enemy has been, is, and will be defeated, and it is our duty to remind him of this very important fact.

If you have been involved in any type of witchcraft, don't think that it is too late to be delivered from it, or to be forgiven. God is ready and willing to forgive you, cleanse you, and totally set you free from the effects of witchcraft. The scripture declares that God is *faithful and just to forgive us our sins and to cleanse us from all unrighteousness* (1 John 1:9). Satan's attack is not about you, it's about his competition with God. His goal is to attack the children of God, and to take captive as many as he can into his dark kingdom.

However, I must re-emphasize that it is our duty to remind him that he was defeated on Calvary, and will be defeated again after the marriage of the Lamb. While on earth, we, the children of God, have been given power through the Holy Ghost (Acts 1:8); with weapons that are *mighty through God to the pulling down of strongholds* (2 Corinthians 10:4). We must take up the whole armor of God, which includes truth, righteousness, peace, faith, salvation, prayer and most of all, the Word of God; because it is with the Word that wc can resist the devil (see Jesus' example in Matthew 4). If we stay consistent in these things, the enemy cannot place strongholds in our lives. *Thanks be to God, which giveth us the victory through our Lord Jesus Christ* (2 Corinthians 10:57).

****

LESSON REVIEW

1. What is witchcraft? Where was its birthplace? Why was this place built (give the two reasons mentioned in the lesson)? Give scripture references.

2. What scripture suggests that ventriloquism originated in the Bible?

3. What type of person is more susceptible to mysticism?

4. Name three forms of modern-day witchcraft.

5. From what class of people did Halloween originate?

6. Name the three major components of witchcraft. Which of these components can drive a person to the point of murder?

Scripture references:

Deuteronomy 18:9-12
Mark 5:1-13; 13:22-23
John 8:32, 44
1 Corinthians 10:18-21
Ephesians 6:11-18; 4:27

1 Timothy 4:1
1 Peter 5:8
Hebrews 9:27
1 John 4:18; 1:9
Revelation 16:13-14; 12:9
Genesis 11:1-9; 1:14-15; 30:27; 44:5,15
1 Samuel 28:7-20
Isaiah 8:19; 2:6; 47:9, 12-13
Micah 5:12
Psalms 139:2; 19:1; 58:5
Daniel 2; 1:20; 4:7; 5:7,11,15; 3:4-25
Matthew 12:38-39; 16:1-3; 4
Numbers 23:23; 24:1
Ecclesiastes 10:11
Judges 16:4-6,15-17
Acts 1:8
2 Corinthians 10:4,57

The Day I Got Set Free

My Diary of Deliverance

The weapons of our warfare are not carnal, but mighty through God to the pulling down of strongholds. (**1 Cor. 10:4**)

Date: _____

- ☐ Monday
- ☐ Tuesday
- ☐ Wednesday
- ☐ Thursday
- ☐ Friday
- ☐ Saturday
- ☐ Sunday

**If two of you shall agree on earth as touching any thing that they shall ask, it shall be done for them. (*Matthew 18:19*)

Today Lord I set myself in agreement with Bishop George Bloomer and the mighty prayer warriors of Bethel Family Worship Center that this yoke will be destroyed in my life, in Jesus' name. Amen

_____

_____

_____

_____

_____

LESSON 10: What is Witchcraft?

LESSON 10: What is Witchcraft?

_____

_____

_____

_____

_____

_____

_____

_____

_____

_____

_____

_____

_____

_____

_____

_____

_____

_____

LESSON

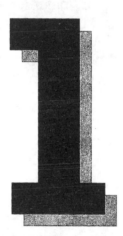

RELIGIOUS DEMONS

¹⁵It is no great thing therefore if his ministers also fashion themselves as ministers of righteousness, whose end shall be according to their works.
—2 Corinthians 11:15

INTRODUCTION

The religious demons are probably the most dangerous group of demons. They seek to promote false religion and false worship. They are possibly the most crafty and subtle demons. They work to develop other religions, but their major focus is tripping up the saints of God. The religious demon can almost always be found in the company of seducing spirits and perverse spirits. These spirits aid the religious demon in its task.

Prayer

Lord Jesus,

Free me from the spirit of religiosity. Help me to be real in my relationship with You and with others around me. I do not want to be a hypocrite in any sense of the Word. I want to walk closely with You, with Your help—leading and guiding me every step of the way. Thank You for Your grace. Amen.

LESSON

WHAT ARE RELIGIOUS DEMONS?

Religious *Threskos* (Greek) – meaning ceremonious in worship; to be pious. (2357 Strong's)

Pious Marked by conspicuous devotion; Marked by false devotion; solemnly hypocritical.

Demon A devil or evil being; an unclean spirit that possesses and afflicts a person, a force or passion.

Seducing spirit An unclean spirit or evil being that paves the way for greater bondage. His purpose is to entice, tempt, attract, fascinate, sear the conscience and win over his victim. Once he has achieved his mission and the victim is bound, he invites other spirits such as the religious demon and the spirit of perversion in to do the work. (I Timothy 4:1)

So, a religious demon could be defined as an evil being or unclean spirit whose purpose is to promote false worship and false devotion.

WHAT VEHICLES DO RELIGIOUS DEMONS USE FOR THEIR PURPOSE?

Vehicles of Religious Demons

1. Idolatry
2. Tradition
3. FalseApostle/Teachers/Doctrines

Let's go to the Word of God as we explore and expose the vehicles used by religious demons.

1. **IDOLATRY:** The worship of idols. Blind or excessive adoration or devotion.

Deuteronomy 32:16-17:
[16]They provoked Him to jealousy with strange gods, with abominations provoked they him to anger.
[17]They sacrificed unto devils, not to God; to gods whom they know not, to new gods that came newly up, whom your fathers feared not.

II Chronicles 33:3-4 (also verses 5-9)
[3]For he (Manasseh) *built again the high places which Hezekiah his father had broken down, and he reared up*

altars for Baalim, and made groves, and worshipped all the host of heaven, and served them.
[4]Also he built altars in the house of the LORD, where of the LORD had said, In Jerusalem shall my name be for ever.

These scriptures are so significant because they do not refer to the pagan nations as being idolaters. In these passages, it is the house of God, Israel, that is doing the idol worship. The demon of religion works diligently with the spirits of seduction and perversion to lure the people of God to idols.

King Manasseh had no regard for his father Hezekiah's obedience to the things of God. He not only worshipped idol gods, but had the audacity to build altars in the Holy place and Most Holy place (read verses 5-9). Intoxicated with the demon of religion and the spirit of seduction, Manasseh sacrificed his children to the fire in the valley of the son of Hinnom (verse 6). He observed times, consulted familiar spirits and wizards, and used enchantments and witchcraft (verse 6). Being king, he caused his people to err and stray from the true God.

Idolatry was prevalent amongst the people of God in both the Old and the New Testaments. Paul is seen in Acts 17:22-23 addressing the Athenians:

[22] *...Ye men of Athens, I perceive that in all things ye are too superstitious.* [23] *For as I passed by, and beheld your devotions, I found an altar with this inscription,* TO THE UNKNOWN GOD. *Whom therefore ye ignorantly worship, him declare I unto you.*

The Amplified Version uses the term *most religious* (very reverent to demons), but I also like the word *superstitious* used in the King James Version. It means *a belief held in spite of evidence to the contrary.* It also means *a practice, belief or rite resulting from faith in magic or chance.* Magic and chance have everything to do with that which is demonically inspired. In God, there is His miraculous power, not magic, and nothing is left to chance, for God is the God of serendipity. What looks like chance to you is actually predestinated by God (Ephesians 1: 4-5).

Today, if Christians were asked whether or not they worshipped idols, there would quickly come the response, "No!" They have no statues of Buddha, no pictures of Hale Salse hanging on their walls and no rosary beads lying around in their drawers, so many Christians would feel confident in their response; however, the religious demon has become even more creative in this age and has peddled idolatry to us in others ways. Without even thinking, we put our jobs, homes, cars, spouses, church buildings and pastors before God. Many times when these things have been taken from us, through some calamity, we truly see the supreme stature in which we have held them. Anything that takes the supreme position (that only God is entitled to hold) in your life is IDOLATRY; and the religious demon has been successful in luring many of us in this area.

WHAT IS GOD'S RESPONSE TO IDOLATRY?

3 Thou shalt have no other gods before me.
4Thou shalt not make unto thee any graven image, or any likeness of any thing that is in heaven above, or that is in the earth beneath, or that is in the water under the earth.
5Thou shalt not bow down thyself to them, nor serve them: for I the LORD thy God am a jealous God, visiting the iniquity of the fathers upon the children unto the third and fourth generation of them that hate me;
6And shewing mercy unto thousands of them that love me, and keep my commandments.
—Exodus 20:3-6

2. **TRADITION:** A mode of thought or behavior followed by a people continuously, from generation to generation; custom or usage. A body of unwritten religious precepts. A time honored practice or a set of such practices.

3But he answered and said unto them, Why do ye also transgress the commandment of God by your tradition?

6And honour not his father or his mother, he shall be free. Thus have ye made the commandment of God of none effect by your tradition.

— Matthew 15:3,6

3For the Pharisees, and all the Jews, except they wash their hands oft, eat not, holding the tradition of the elders.

5Then the Pharisees and scribes asked him, Why walk not thy disciples according to the tradition of the elders, but eat bread with unwashen hands?

8For laying aside the commandment of God, ye hold the tradition of men, as the washing of pots and cups: and many other such like things ye do.

⁹And he said unto them, Full well ye reject the commandment of God, that ye may keep your own tradition.

¹³Making the word of God of none effect through your tradition, which ye have delivered: and many such like things do ye.
—Mark 7:3,5,8-9,13

The Pharisees and Sadducees considered themselves to be very devout men. These men had studied the scriptures and were considered scholars of their time. They wore the best robes and ate in the best restaurants. They spent their time debating scripture, giving long public prayers and fasting openly. These men daily studied the scriptures, yet added laborious rituals to tax the people; preventing the people from seeing a true view of God and the relationship He was calling His people to with Him. These men considered themselves to be holy, set apart, and without blemish, but Second Timothy 3:5 and Isaiah 29:13 give light to the true condition of these men.

⁵Having a form of godliness, but denying the power thereof: from such turn away.
—2 Timothy 3:5

13Wherefore the Lord said, Forasmuch as this people draw near me with their mouth, and with their lips do honour me, but have removed their heart far from me, and their fear toward me is taught by the precept of men:

—Isaiah 29:13

When the religious demon cannot ensnare us with idolatry outright (because these men were idol worshipers, worshipping themselves and their acquired intellects), he uses theologies and philosophies, which develop into doctrines of devils and religious traditions. He then uses these weapons to move us away from the truths of God's Word and His fellowship. It becomes so easy for us, as it was for them, to make false interpretations of scripture that will support our cause, leaving us bound in religious practices and traditions. Some of the modern-day traditions and practices include the following, which hinder and bind the children of God:

1. Women should not wear pants.
2. Christians should not wear jewelry or make-up.
3. Christians should not consult a doctor.
4. All Christians should be vegetarians.

These are just some of the doctrines that have come out of the misinterpretation of scripture. The religious demon and the perverse spirit are all too happy to indulge man, and to lead him astray–into great bondage.

The Pharisees and Saducees are not the only ones holding tight to their traditions or sacred calves. Think for a moment. How many times have you seen individuals' sacred calves being slain by the Word of God, yet they still refused to surrender that which was now pronounced dead? Because they were taught something for years and years, they now refuse to let go of that false teaching, despite the revelation of the true Word, which is lain before them to refute and cut asunder every false doctrine.

What people are actually saying is that tradition is more important than God's truths. Does this mean that you have to accept something as being true just because the Word is being presented to support it before you are able to search it out for yourself? No, the Word of God says in Second Timothy 2:15 that we must *study to show* ourselves *approved unto God, a workman that needeth not to be ashamed, rightly dividing the word of truth.* (Read also Acts 17:10-12).

Paul admonishes the Christian in Colossians 2:8 to *Beware* [be cautious] *lest any man spoil you through philosophy and vain deceit, after the tradition of men, after the rudiments of the world, and not after Christ.* We would do well to heed (pay attention) to Paul's warning to the church of Colosse.

3. FALSE APOSTLES/ TEACHERS/DOCTRINES

False: Contrary to fact or truth. Arising from mistaken ideas. Resembling but not properly or accurately designated as such.

Apostle: One who leads or advocates a cause or movement.

Teacher: One who imparts knowledge or skill to; give instruction to. To cause to learn by example or experience. Instruct, educate tutor, train, school or discipline.

Doctrine: Something that is taught. A principle or body or principles presented for acceptance or belief, as by a religious, political, scientific, or philosophic group; dogma.

[13]For such are false apostles, deceitful workers, transforming themselves into the apostles of Christ.
[14]And no marvel; for Satan himself is transformed into an angel of light.

15Therefore it is no great thing if his ministers also be transformed as the ministers of righteousness; whose end shall be according to their works.

—II Corinthians 11: 13 –15

1Beloved, believe not every spirit, but try the spirits whether they are of God: because many false prophets are gone out into the world.
2Hereby know ye the Spirit of God: Every spirit that confesseth that Jesus Christ is come in the flesh is of God:
3And every spirit that confesseth not that Jesus Christ is come in the flesh is not of God: and this is that spirit of antichrist, whereof ye have heard that it should come; and even now already is it in the world.

—I John 4:1-3

1But there were false prophets also among the people, even as there shall be false teachers among you, who privily shall bring in damnable here-sies, even denying the Lord that bought them, and bring upon them-selves swift destruction.
2And many shall follow their perni-cious (causing great harm) *ways; by*

*reason of whom the way of truth shall
be evil spoken of.*
—II Peter 2:1-2

Satan is wreaking havoc on the church of God
because many churches have refused to pay
attention to and act upon scripture. Christians
are not trying the spirits to see whether they
are of God. The Christian community, although
hungry for the supernatural and that which is
spectacular, has become at ease in Zion, and
has accepted, as a gift from God, anyone who
appears to be spiritual and possesses the
ability to move in the supernatural. Many
Christians believe that because these people
use the terms *Jesus*, *Lord* or *Christ*, that they
are reverencing the Lord and Savior of the
Holy Bible, but this is not always true. Satan's
stratagem in these latter days is deception, and
who better to deceive than those who worship
the True and Living God. This is the enemy's
main objective.

Maybe you are saying right now, "It's not
possible. I am saved!" The Word of God says,
if it were possible he [Satan] would *deceive the
very elect* (Matthew 24:24). Maybe you are
saying, "The Word says, *if* it were possible."
Do not be secure in this thinking. The only
reason the *very elect* are not deceived is
because they have studied the Word of God,
line upon line and precept upon precept. They
have accepted what the Word has to say and

allowed tradition to die when necessary. The very elect have hidden the Word of God in their hearts that they might not sin against Him. In other words, they have prepared.

INSTITUTIONALIZED DECEPTION

In the pursuit of social status and financial betterment, many have been misled by joining organizations without having the full knowledge and understanding of the history or purpose of those institutions.

> *[14]Be ye not unequally yoked together with unbelievers: for what fellowship hath righteousness with unrighteous- ness? and what communion hath light with darkness?*
> *[15]And what concord hath Christ with Belial? or what part hath he that believeth with an infidel?*
> *[16]And what agreement hath the temple of God with idols? for ye are the temple of the living God; as God hath said, I will dwell in them, and walk in them; and I will be their God, and they shall be my people.*
> *[17]Wherefore come out from among them, and be ye separate, saith the Lord, and touch not the unclean thing; and I will receive you,*

¹⁸And will be a Father unto you, and ye shall be my sons and daughters, saith the Lord Almighty.

—II Corinthians 6: 14 - 18

Masonry organizations, as well as many sororities and fraternities, are oftentimes very attractive because of the benefits attached to its memberships. And because of their "family-oriented" values, they tend to draw to them those looking for a well-rounded and spiritually motivated institution in which to belong.

Little do most know, however, the history and non-spiritual aspects that many of these organizations have also inherited.

□ **FREE MASONS**

The masons, who worked on any public works, as well as some of the great medieval cathedrals, were indeed "free masons." They were known to establishes lodges wherever they came together to work. Originally, the lodges served two purposes:

1. A place of lodging (somewhere for them to stay)
2. A meeting place (their headquarters)

One text dates the origin of the masons back to the Tower of Babel. Still, there seems to be no clear indication of God—The Supreme Being that Christians worship as the same God that the members of this organization are required to believe in—only that they must acknowledge "a" Supreme Being. Likewise, many of their secretive rituals and symbols are questionable as it relates to Christian beliefs and biblical principles.

❑ FRATERNITIES AND SORORITIES

Other secretive organizations, such as fraternities and sororities, are also questionable; and the practices of many of these institutions are blatantly against the teachings and commands of biblical instruction. Because of their contacts and influence over people in our society, it has been said that Black fraternities and sororities are even more powerful than the Black church. Many of them observe and place Greek gods and goddesses on their emblems. Others go as far as branding the skin, which Leviticus 19:28 warns:

Ye shall not make any cuttings in your flesh for the dead, nor print any marks upon you: I am the Lord.

It has been documented that physical and mental hazing is sometimes imposed upon those being initiated into the organizations. Hazing has been defined as any willful act directed against any student for the purpose of causing:

1. Humiliation
2. Intimidation
3. Social banishment
4. Shame or disgrace
5. The stifling of ambition
6. Fear

While many innocently join these organizations and others, they must recognize that these institutions are not Christian-based and have no biblical functions.

HOW CAN WE TELL THE DIFFERENCE BETWEEN THE WORK OF THE HOLY SPIRIT AND THAT OF A RELIGIOUS SPIRIT OR UNHOLY DEMON?

HOLY SPIRIT	RELIGIOUS DEMON (UNHOLY)
1. God almighty with unlimited power and knowledge.	1. A limited, created being with knowledge superior only to humans, but limited.
2. Pure and holy and brings these attributes into the person in whom He abides—power to overcome sin.	2. Is full of corruption and leads the person in whom he dwells into deeper sin.
3. Always brings glory to Jesus, thereby imparts humility into the person in whom He resides.	3. Glorifies the person in whom he resides, drawing attention to man and away from God; thus imparting pride.
4. Never blanks out our	4. Frequently blanks out

minds. He desires our cooperation with Him. (2 Cor. 10:5; Phil. 2:13)	the minds of his host and works best with his victims while they are passive.
5. We cannot control Him, but He works when and in whatever way He pleases. (1 Cor. 12:11)	5. Deceives his victims into believing that they can control him.
6. Gives the desire to read the Bible.	6.Provides distractions to keep his victims from reading the Bible.
7. Helps us to understand the scriptures.	7. Brings confusion to his victims as they read the scriptures (2 Cor. 11:3).

Conclusion

These are just some of the ways one can tell the difference between the Holy Spirit and a religious demon. However, I admonish you to diligently study the scriptures for yourself, develop a real one on one relationship with God, stop being so quick to always seek another person to help you out of your situations, and take time daily to seek God concerning the deceptions of the enemy. Don't allow the religious demons of our modern day to deceive you into engaging in ungodly acts or rituals. Neither be deceived by the traditions of men which come to bind you under the fist of authority and stifle the Word of God. Remember, *a wise man will hear, and will increase learning; and a man of understanding shall*

239

attain unto wise counsel (Proverbs 1:5). The very elect were not deceived only because they hid the Word in their hearts. What are you hiding in your heart? And is it enough to bring about victory in your life?

****

LESSON REVIEW

1. Name the vehicles of religious demons.

2. Name four traditions still used in the church.

3. Name two institutions discussed in this lesson.

4. What institution branched out from the Masons?

5. The Holy Spirit helps us to _____ the scriptures, but the religious demon brings _____ to his victims as they read the scriptures.

Scripture References:

2 Corinthians 11:13-15
1 Timothy 4:1; 1:4
Deuteronomy 32:16-17
2 Chronicles 33:3-9
Acts 17:22-23
Ephesians 1:4-5
Exodus 20:3-6
Matthew 15:3-6; 24:24
Mark 7:3,5,8-9,13
2 Timothy 3:5; 1:7; 2:15
Isaiah 29:13

The Day I Got Set Free

My Diary of Deliverance

The weapons of our warfare are not carnal, but mighty through God to the pulling down of strongholds. (1 Cor. 10:4)

Date: _____

- ☐ Monday
- ☐ Tuesday
- ☐ Wednesday
- ☐ Thursday
- ☐ Friday
- ☐ Saturday
- ☐ Sunday

**If two of you shall agree on earth as touching any thing that they shall ask, it shall be done for them. (Matthew 18:19)

Today Lord I set myself in agreement with Bishop George Bloomer and the mighty prayer warriors of Bethel Family Worship Center that this yoke will be destroyed in my life, in Jesus' name. Amen

_____

_____

_____

_____

_____

LESSON 11: Religious Demons

_____

_____

_____

_____

_____

_____

_____

_____

_____

_____

_____

_____

_____

_____

_____

_____

_____

_____

_____

_____

LESSON 11: Religious Demons

_____

_____

_____

_____

_____

_____

_____

_____

_____

_____

_____

_____

_____

_____

_____

_____

_____

_____

_____

LESSON

IDENTIFYING & BREAKING GENERA-
TIONAL CURSES

As the bird by wandering, as the swallow by flying, so the curse causeless shall not come. —Proverbs 26:1-2

INTRODUCTION

There is clearly no curse without a cause.

CURSES open the door to demonic spirits, giving them legal entry into a person's life. In the case of a *generational curse*, the demonic force uses this opportunity to afflict entire families throughout many generations. Generational curses originate from an iniquitous spirit that was passed down.

Prayer

Lord Jesus,

Now that I've recognized the doors that the enemy uses to draw us into the demonic, I further close these doors by renouncing every demonic curse and generational curse in the name of Jesus. I declare my spiritual liberty; for Christ has redeemed us from the curse of the law (Galatians 3:13). The Word also says that he whom the Son sets free is free indeed (John 8:36). I am free from this day forth in Jesus' name. Amen.

LESSON

Curse: Evil or misfortune that comes as if in response to imprecation or as retribution.

We have an adversary who seeks to destroy us. Demons can cause physical disease or mental suffering. The Bible teaches that Satan and his demons are the source of sin and disease. They spread sin and disease and control the law of sin and death in the human race. When resistance to these powers is delayed, time and opportunity gain a strong-hold, which becomes difficult to dislodge. It's important to realize that God should immediately be sought to overcome these attacks and avoid long sieges of defeat.

One of the greatest battles Christians confront is the battle of the mind. As illustrated in the parable of Mark 4:1-9 where the word is sowed in the heart of man and the enemy wrestles to steal the Word. The enemy is cunning and knows the biological make up of mankind, as he *thinketh in his heart so is he.* So the enemy tries his best to plant discouragement, rejection, envy, anger, pride, lying, wicked imaginations in the heart of man, touching every area of life to control the mind to destruction.

There is a possibility of being cursed without being oppressed, possessed, or depressed by a spirit. A curse is normally something that was spoken against you that you have become convinced that you must live with. This, however, is not true. Though there may be a cause for the curse, the individual does not have to live with the curse. The curse can be broken through speaking the Word, denouncing it, and confessing what God says instead.

EXAMPLES OF GENERATIONAL CURSES

- Adam & Eve (work is a curse – Genesis Chapter Three)
- Cain
- The Children of Israel

4 THINGS THAT OPEN YOU TO A CURSE

- Bad Counsel
- Disobedience
- Rejecting the Word of God
- Accepting the curse spoken over your life from another individual

EVIDENCE OF A CURSE

- Mental & Emotional Breakdown
- Being Accident Prone
- Having Multiple Miscarriages
- Reoccurring sickness
- Heavy and Continual Thoughts of Suicide
- Financial debt, despite adequate income

NO CURSE WITHOUT A CAUSE

☐ ADAM & EVE

Cause: Disobedience (they both ate of the tree of the knowledge of good and evil)
Curse: Work – Adam's curse (work is a curse)

> *[17]And unto Adam he said, Because thou hast hearkened unto the voice of thy wife, and hast eaten of the tree, of which I commanded thee, saying, Thou shalt not eat of it: cursed is the ground for thy sake; in sorrow shalt thou eat of it all the days of thy life;*
> *[18]Thorns also and thistles shall it bring forth to thee; and thou shalt eat the herb of the field;*
> *[19]In the sweat of thy face shalt thou eat bread, till thou return unto the ground...*
> —Genesis 3:17-19

☐ CAIN

Cause: Murder (killed his brother)
Curse: The curse of poverty (he is cursed from the earth)

*Generational curse passed down from his father, Adam. They were both punished with curses of the ground.

⁹And the Lord said unto Cain, Where is Abel thy brother? And he said, I know not: Am I my brother's keeper?
¹⁰And he said, What hast thou done? the voice of thy brother's blood crieth unto me from the ground.
¹¹And now art thou cursed from the earth, which hath opened her mouth to receive thy brother's blood from thy hand;
¹²When thou tillest the ground, it shall not henceforth yield unto thee her strength; a fugitive and a vagabond shalt thou be in the earth.
—Genesis 4:9-12

□ **THE CHILDREN OF ISRAEL**

Cause: disobedience and unbelief
Curse: made to wander in the wilderness and not allowed to reach the Promised Land

³²But as for you, your carcases, they shall fall in this wilderness.
³³And your children shall wander in the wilderness forty years, and bear your whoredoms, until your carcases be wasted in the wilderness.
³⁵I the Lord have said, I will surely do it unto all this evil congregation, that are gathered together against me: in this wilderness they shall be consumed, and there they shall die.

Conclusion

Curses never occur without a cause. They occur because of bad counsel, disobedience, rejecting the Word of God, and accepting curses spoken over one's life from others. Curses are evidenced by multiple miscarriages and accidents, reoccurring sicknesses, constant thoughts of suicide, and mental and emotional breakdown. One can become cursed without being oppressed, possessed or depressed by an evil spirit.

After examining the evidences of a curse, and the things that can open you up to a curse, some of you may recognize a curse in your own lives. There is no need to be dismayed, however, as stated, curses can be broken. Simply speak the Word, denounce the curse, and confess what God says about you! God has power to reverse curses to His glory.

> *...but the LORD thy God turned the curse into a blessing unto thee, because the LORD thy God loved thee.*
> —Deuteronomy 23:4b

LESSON REVIEW

1. Where do curses originate?

2. Name three examples of generational curses.

3. Name two evidences of a curse.

4. Name five things that can open one up to a curse.

5. Work is a _____.

Scripture References:

Proverbs 26:1-2
Galatians 3:13
John 8:36
Mark 4:1-9
Genesis 3:17-19; 4:9-12
Numbers 14:32-33, 35
Deuteronomy 23:4b

The Day I Got Set Free

My Diary of Deliverance

*The weapons of our warfare are not carnal, but mighty
through God to the pulling down of strongholds. (1 Cor.
10:4)*

Date: _____

- ❑ Monday
- ❑ Tuesday
- ❑ Wednesday
- ❑ Thursday
- ❑ Friday
- ❑ Saturday
- ❑ Sunday

***If two of you shall agree on earth as touching any thing
that they shall ask, it shall be done for them. (Matthew
18:19)*

*Today Lord I set myself in agreement with
Bishop George Bloomer and the mighty prayer
warriors of Bethel Family Worship Center that
this yoke will be destroyed in my life, in Jesus'
name. Amen*

_____

_____

_____

_____

_____

255

_____

_____

_____

_____

_____

_____

_____

_____

_____

_____

_____

_____

_____

_____

_____

_____

_____

_____

_____

LESSON 12: Identifying and Breaking Generational Curses

_____

_____

_____

_____

_____

_____

_____

_____

_____

_____

_____

_____

_____

_____

_____

_____

_____

_____

_____

_____

_____

_____

_____

_____

_____

_____

_____

_____

_____

_____

_____

_____

_____

_____

_____

_____

_____

_____

_____

_____

_____

_____

LESSON

13

HOW TO REJECT REJECTION

And he beheld them, and said, What is this then that is written, The stone which the builders rejected, the same is become the head of the corner?
—Luke 20:17

Reject: to refuse to accept, consider, submit to, take for some purpose or use; to refuse to hear, receive, or admit; rebuff repel; to cast off

INTRODUCTION

A person suffering from rejection feels unaccepted, can have low self esteem, and spend a large portion of his or her life trying to find somewhere to "fit in," and **making** a way to fit in areas that he or she does not belong, all because of the oppressive force of rejection. Rejection is a cycle, normally transferred by other rejected individuals.

Rejection can normally be traced to a person's past. Even infants who are born can feel the rejection that their mothers may have felt while carrying them, and may cry a lot, or grow up to feel rejected if the vicious cycle of rejection is not cured.

Rejection seeks attention. Rejection connects you with the spirit of sensuality, and sensuality causes you to live in a state of nudity. Nudity and the wearing of seductive clothing have everything to do with an oppressive spirit that is on you. Rejection is an oppressive force that can be transferred through conversation, through letters, through videos, and so on. Rejection causes one to lose focus and allows other less important things to take precedence over God and the things of God. Consequently, a person can't enter total worship until first making some sacrifices. This means that God must be placed before those things that are used to fill the void, which was caused by rejection.

Prayer

Lord Jesus,

You were, and are, not always received of men. Your Word says that You were despised and rejected of men (Isaiah 53:3). You know first hand about rejection, and we ask You to give us the full revelation of it. Show us the signs, symptoms, and effects of it. Show us how we can be healed and set free from it; then show us how to remain free from it. Reassure us that as long as we are accepted by You, we are accepted by the One who matters most of all. Thank You. Amen.

LESSON

THE FATHERLESS CHILD

The presence and stability of the male voice must be present in a child's life, especially around children who are fatherless, because rejection can be transferred to children through what is spoken to them. Growing up, my father and his mother (my grandmother) planted the seed in my mind that I was "retarded," and I was even placed in a class with other mentally handicapped children at my school. There was one occasion where my grandmother placed me in the middle of the floor and told me that I was going to learn to tie my shoes. Every time I tied the lace into a knot instead of a bow, she'd smack my hand...*wham* ... as she again reminded me of how "retarded" I was. Then, with sore fingers, I tried, at her demand, to get the knot out of the shoelace. This lasted all day long with my grandmother hovering over me; yet, I still could not get it right.

A LESSON IN LOVE

When my grandmother finally stepped away and went into another room, my sister Cynthia came to my aid.

"George," she said, "this is how you tie your shoes," she kept demonstrating to me, as she wept at the same time.

As my sister began to cry, I asked her, "What are you crying for?"

She responded, "Because I don't want her to hit you anymore."

At those final words of compassion, I reached down and finally tied my shoe. It was my sister's motivation and act of kindness, not my grandmother's brute force and intimidating tactics, that eventually gave me the understanding of making a loop instead of a knot, equipping me with the ability to finally tie my shoe. I found in that instant that my sister Cynthia was in more torment than I was over the fact that I could not tie my shoe, and because I knew that she was rooting for me, I was then motivated to finally get it right. My sister Cynthia was an amazing individual who constantly went into battle for all of her siblings. Even when my mother was spanking us too much, it was Cynthia who stepped in to hold back my mother's hand, while yelling to the rest of the children to run, knowing that my mother would turn on her instead and invoke her brute punishment with even more force.

IT'S A SPIRITUAL FIGHT

Bitterness can cause a person to lose the fight associated with rejection. Low self-esteem and bitterness causes one's human nature to instinctively want to lash out at someone, seek revenge, make those closest to us pay for the hurts invoked on us by others and so on. The best weapon, however, is prayer and a willingness to live according to the word of God. This outline is shown in Matthew 5:44-48.

1) Pray for your enemies or those who may have transferred to you a spirit of rejection.

But I say unto you, Love your enemies, bless them that curse you, do good to them that hate you, and pray for them which despitefully use you, and persecute you;
That ye may be the children of your Father which is in heaven: for he maketh his sun to rise on the evil and on the good, and sendeth rain on the just and on the unjust.

What good is it then, to hate and pray for God to destroy those who've rejected you and spoken evil of you? God rains on the just as well as the unjust. If He does decide to avenge our enemies, that is His decision, and not one that we should make for ourselves.

2) Show love to all.

For if ye love them which love you, what reward have ye? do not even the publicans the same?
And if ye salute your brethren only, what do ye more than others? Do not even the publicans so?

Even the sinners can show love to and salute with sincerity those who love them back, but it is a true believer who can love

his enemy or show kindness to one who has oppressed him. That is the challenge.

3) Be without blame.

Be ye therefore perfect, even as your Father which is in heaven is perfect.

The Greek word for "perfect" is "teleios" which means complete. Perfect in this sense is not to be translated as our modern usage, which means being entirely without fault—a sinless life—but instead, "perfect," in this text refers to a life that is complete in the Lord and submitted to His will.

That ye may stand perfect and complete in all the will of God. (Col. 4:12)

JEPHTHAH THE GILEADITE WAS REJECTED
(JUDGES 11:1-11)

Jephthah the Gileadite was a mighty man of valor, but he was also the son of a harlot. When his father's sons grew up, they threw Jephthah out and said to him, *Thou shalt not inherit in our father's house; for thou art the son of a strange woman.* When the children of Ammon made war against Israel, however, the elders of Gilead *went to fetch Jephthah out of the land of Tob* so that he could help them fight against the children of Ammon.

And they said unto Jephthah, Come, and be our captain, that we may fight with the children of Ammon.

And Jephthah said unto the elders of Gilead, Did not ye hate me, and expel me out of my father's house? And why are ye come unto me now when ye are in distress?

And the elders of Gilead said unto Jephthah, Therefore we turn again to thee now, that thou mayest go with us, and fight against the children of Ammon, and be our head over all the inhabitants of Gilead.

And Jephthah said unto the elders of Gilead, If ye bring me home again to fight against the children of Ammon, and the Lord deliver them before me, shall I be your head?

And the elders of Gilead said unto Jephthah, The Lord be witness between us, if we do not so according to thy words.

Then Jephthah went with the elders of Gilead, and the people made him head and captain over them: and Jephtha uttered all his words before the Lord in Mizpeh.

Jephthah became his enemies' answer as they were forced to go out and "fetch" that which they had "thrust out."

A Valuable Principle: Behave yourself today, because you don't know who or what you're going to be tomorrow.

If Jephthah had taken vengeance upon his brothers, he may have been killed. He would have aborted his own spiritual destiny. But because he fled from them and allowed patience to have her perfect work, he was able to now free his oppressors from those who now oppressed him.

Hebrew: *Jephthah* means *He* [God] *will open.*

Because Jephthah allowed patience to have her perfect work, God opened the door for him to deliver his people and become head over them.

Conclusion

Remember, no matter what you've gone through or what you're currently going through, continue to go to church, worship the Lord, and communicate with Him and God will heal you. After He heals you, He's going to use you and people will begin to thank God for you. Then, your scars will become your medals. Whatever hurts and pains exist in your life, work extremely hard to get over them. Don't spend a lot of time crying and brooding over past hurts. Remember that someone else is waiting for you to get delivered so that your testimony can be the vessel that God uses as their deliverance. You are someone else's deliverance, so get healed. Don't ever cease to worship God through whatever you're going through, and don't ever cut off your communication to the Father.

You can't have warfare without worship. You will experience peace through worship and see the hand of God upon your children like you've never seen before. Truly, the spirit of "father-lessness" can be placed under the fist of the spoken Word and destroyed. Fatherlessness is the number one cause of children wetting the bed; and the number one cause of pregnancy is rejection—women doing anything to gain a few minutes of pleasure and love, thus giving their bodies to men to feel the temporal illusion of a loving embrace. Let us begin now to stop the cycle!

****

LESSON REVIEW

1. Rejection is a _____ , normally _____ other individuals.

2. Rejection connects you with the spirit of _____ , and _____ causes you to live in a state of _____.

3. Rejection can be transferred to children through _____ _____ _____ _____.

4. The best weapon against rejection is _____.

5. _____ is also closely associated with rejection.

Scripture References:

Luke 20:17
Matthew 5:44-48
Colossians 4:12
Judges 11:1-11

The Day I Got Set Free

My Diary of Deliverance

The weapons of our warfare are not carnal, but mighty through God to the pulling down of strongholds. (**1 Cor. 10:4**)

Date: _____

- ❑ Monday
- ❑ Tuesday
- ❑ Wednesday
- ❑ Thursday
- ❑ Friday
- ❑ Saturday
- ❑ Sunday

**If two of you shall agree on earth as touching any thing that they shall ask, it shall be done for them. (Matthew 18:19)*

Today Lord I set myself in agreement with Bishop George Bloomer and the mighty prayer warriors of Bethel Family Worship Center that this yoke will be destroyed in my life, in Jesus' name. Amen

_____

_____

_____

_____

_____

LESSON 13: How to Reject Rejection

_____

_____

_____

_____

_____

_____

_____

_____

_____

_____

_____

_____

_____

_____

_____

_____

_____

_____

_____

LESSON 13: How to Reject Rejection

_____

_____

_____

_____

_____

_____

_____

_____

_____

_____

_____

_____

_____

_____

_____

_____

_____

_____

_____

_____

_____

_____

LESSON

ADDICTION

No temptation has overtaken you except such as is common to man; but God is faithful, who will not allow you to be tempted beyond what you are able, but with the temptation will also make the way of escape, that you may be able to bear it. —1 Corinthians 10:13

INTRODUCTION

The strategy of Lucifer is to first tempt, then ensnare his victims. Of course the best weapon against temptation is resistance, but those who fall prey to his tactics often find themselves slaves to Lucifer's power of addiction.

1 Corinthians 10:13 lets us know that God will not allow the enemy to tempt any man beyond what he or she is able to bear. And even when the temptation seems unbearable, God will **make** a way for the individual to escape.

Resist the devil and he will flee!

UNDERSTANDING ADDICTION

Addiction - any habitual activity from which a person finds himself incapable of breaking free. It's very hard, it seems, for those who've never been bound by addiction to understand its power and the inability of the bound individual to be set free. Addiction can stem from drug abuse, to demons of lust—not only for sexual pleasures, but also for power, money, fame and so on.

Some addictions can be traced throughout an entire family's genealogical order. Many of us know entire families of alcoholics, drug abusers, and sexual addicts who use illicit and/or lawless means to have their need met or even families who clamor over each other and others as they lust for power—trampling over anyone who gets in their way.

COUNSELING ADDICTS

In counseling someone who suffers from addiction, we must be able to discern timing and know the voice of God. One can easily mistake, for example, a demon for someone whose body is going through the withdrawal symptoms of an abusive substance. A person can only be set free through the power of God. Counseling from man can supply the individual with the information needed for discipline, but ultimately he or she must be led to the Lord for deliverance. It is God, and not man, who sets addicts free!

After an individual has been set free, he or she must make a conscience decision to remain around those who pray and know the Lord, attend church on a regular basis in order to maintain freedom and pray also for oneself.

Don't be judgmental! It has been said that when a person's desire to stop smoking, drinking, abusing drugs, engaging in illicit sexual activities and so on, that they need only to stop, and if they don't stop, it's because they want to remain bound. This is not, however, always the case. When a person is oppressed they are controlled by demonic influences.

WHY DO ADDICTS SEEM TO GET WORSE?

Many times we see addicts who venture in and out of rehabilitation, wanting to be set free, yet not knowing how to maintain that freedom. Instead they oftentimes seem to get worse before they get better.

We are subject to revisit past relationships, addictions, and bad habits. when we are alienated from God through ignorance of His Word. Satan will bring strongholds of our past back into our lives to tempt us.

The bible teaches that if a person is set free and then goes back into bondage, then the demon that once resided with the individual goes out and finds seven more demons worse than the first in order to continue his oppression. Consequently, the individual ends up seven times worse than he was at the initial bondage (See Matthew 12:43-45).

DON'T TOY WITH LUCIFER

Satan is not to be toyed with. We are over-comers through Christ Jesus and that is the attitude that we must take in order to defeat satan and his demonic armed forces. His desire is to turn our will to his will so that he can control our actions (witchcraft). A person suffering from addiction has, at some point, forfeited his or her will to the temptations of Lucifer, allowing him legal reign in a particular area of his or her life. Therefore, it will take more than just will-power for the individual to break free. The bound individual must be dependant upon a higher power, and that power is Jesus Christ. Leaders counseling addicts, must teach this truth!

Satan's Deception
Temptation in Your Weakness
Surrenderance to Temptation
Addiction
Possession

God's Deliverance
Prayer & Intercession
Surrenderance to God
Freedom
Discipline

Conclusion

Addiction is a habitual activity from which a person finds it hard to break free. This is one of Lucifer's greatest desires—to ensnare a person, leaving them weakened to any form of resistance. If one has never been bound by addiction, it's very hard to understand it's power. In counseling, we must be able to discern the timing of God. Symptoms of withdrawal are often mistaken for a demon. Addicts, in many cases, seem to get worse because they have been set free once, but then the demons that once resided within them go out and find seven more demons. They end up seven times worse than when they began their habit. In order to become totally set free, they cannot continue to toy with their deliverance. They must willingly renounce Satan's grip on their lives, and totally depend upon the power of God to do the work.

Deliverance from addiction can be obtained by prayer and intercession, surrenderance to God, and discipline. Using the Word of God to confess what God says about you, and against the devil when he tempts you, is another great way of maintaining your deliverance. For *faith cometh by hearing, and hearing by the Word of God* (Romans 10:17). So confess it aloud so that you can build yourself up in faith, and to announce to the principalities that you intend to remain set free. It's definitely easier said than done, but with consistency and discipline, the stronghold of addiction will one day only be a memory.

LESSON REVIEW

1. Why do addicts seem to get worse? Give the scripture reference that supports this?

2. When counseling an individual, we must learn that it is not by our might, but by what?

3. Some addictions can be traced back to what?

4. An addict must never _____ with Lucifer.

5. Name the four steps of deliverance as given in the lesson.

Scripture Reference:

1 Corinthians 10:13

The Day I Got Set Free

My Diary of Deliverance

The weapons of our warfare are not carnal, but mighty through God to the pulling down of strongholds. (1 Cor. 10:4)

Date: _____

- ❑ Monday
- ❑ Tuesday
- ❑ Wednesday
- ❑ Thursday
- ❑ Friday
- ❑ Saturday
- ❑ Sunday

**If two of you shall agree on earth as touching any thing that they shall ask, it shall be done for them. (Matthew 18:19)

Today Lord I set myself in agreement with Bishop George Bloomer and the mighty prayer warriors of Bethel Family Worship Center that this yoke will be destroyed in my life, in Jesus' name. Amen

_____

_____

_____

_____

_____

LESSON 14: Addiction

_____

_____

_____

_____

_____

_____

_____

_____

_____

_____

_____

_____

_____

_____

_____

_____

_____

_____

_____

_____

_____

_____

_____

_____

_____

_____

_____

_____

_____

_____

_____

_____

_____

_____

_____

_____

_____

LESSON 14: Addiction

_____

_____

_____

_____

_____

_____

_____

_____

_____

_____

_____

_____

_____

_____

_____

_____

_____

_____

_____

LESSON

THE SPIRIT OF PRIDE

In that day the LORD with his sore and great and strong sword shall punish leviathan, the piercing serpent, even leviathan that crooked serpent; and he shall slay the dragon that is in the sea. — Isaiah 27:1

INTRODUCTION

The purpose of this lesson is to identify the characteristics of pride and how Satan uses it to build a false sense of security in the lives of Christians.

Prayer

Lord Jesus,

I thank You, Lord, that as You reveal unto me the spiritual aspects of the deadly force of pride, that You will begin also to free me and keep the spirit of pride from manifesting in my life. Amen.

LESSON

Key Scriptures: Job 41:1, 8-10, 30-34

Pride
Undue sense of one's own superiority; inordinate self-esteem; arrogance; conceit.

Leviathan
A spirit often referred to as a sea monster. Similar to crocodile or sea serpent.

Rejection
Refusal to accept, receive, hear, submit to; to cast off; to throw back.

Lust
Personal pleasure or delight. Intense desire, sexual or otherwise. Intense longing; lasciviousness.

Hurt
To do substantial harm to; damage; cause pain or anguish; to offend; to injure.

Insecurity
Not confident; not sure, shaky; not highly stable or well-adjusted (caused by fear and anxiety)

Shame
Painful emotion caused by a consciousness of guilt.
Shortcoming; condition of humiliation, disgrace; something that brings strong regret.

Fear
Unpleasant strong emotion caused by an anticipation or awareness of danger. Reason for alarm.

Self-righteousness
Convinced of one's own righteousness in contrast with the actions and beliefs of others.

Religious spirits
Promote false religion and false worship. They work to trip the saints of God often found accompanied by seducing and perverse spirits.

QUESTIONS TO JOB

In Job 41:1-7, God questions Job and makes a series of comments, which can be related to the Leviathan spirit. From these questions, the characteristics of Leviathan are revealed.

1. Will he make many supplications unto thee? will he speak soft words unto thee?

—Job 41:3

RESPONSE:
"No, he will not humble himself and make supplication."

Supplication is a form of prayer. Leviathan hinders prayer. Refusing to pray, becoming sleepy in prayer, and finding it difficult to pray, are all manifestations of Leviathan. Pride does not sense the need to pray. Pride will not seek God, because pride will not pray.

2. Will he make a covenant with thee? wilt thou take him for a servant for ever?

—Job 41:4

RESPONSE:
"No, he will not make a covenant with thee or be a servant."

Leviathan is independent. He will never submit and serve another. Marriage is a covenant. Whether you are the bride of Christ or of man, pride dishonors covenants. Fornicators dishonor covenants. Adulterers dishonor covenants. Pride blinds us from receiving the benefits of our covenant through the blood of Jesus.

Some of the benefits of salvation are healing, deliverance from bondage, natural and spiritual prosperity, gifts of the spirit, miracles, and the baptism of the Holy Ghost. When a believer has a problem with walking in the fullness of God... check for Leviathan.

3. By his neesings a light doth shine, and his eyes are like the eyelids of the morning.
   Out of his mouth go burning lamps, and sparks of fire leap out.
                                    —Job 41:18-19

RESPONSE:
"Leviathan is a fire-breathing dragon."

Even so the tongue is a little member, and boasteth great things. Behold how great a matter a little fire kindleth. And the tongue is a fire, a world of iniquity:

291

so is the tongue among our members,
that it defiled the whole body, and

setteth on fire the course of nature;
and it is set on fire of hell.
—James 3:5,6

Fire spreads, and is a destructive force. For the lake of hell is prepared with fire and brimstone. The grace of God and a clean heart will help sustain us from Leviathan.

4. In his neck remaineth strength, and sorrow is turned into joy before him.

—Job 41:22

RESPONSE:
In his neck remaineth strength...

His strength is in his neck. A strong neck means stubbornness, rebellion, and stiff-necked. Stubbornness is the refusal to change. *Rebellion is as the sin of witchcraft* (1 Samuel 15:23). Stubbornness will cause you to reject the Word of God. King Saul is a good example. God called the children of Israel stiff-necked people. We cannot grow without change. Refusing to hear, not being submissive, and remaining unteachable are the fruits of a stiff-necked person.

5. *His heart is as firm as a stone; yea, as*

hard as a piece of the nether millstone.
—Job 41:24

RESPONSE:
"Leviathan is hard-hearted."

Hard as a rock. A hard heart is the cause of division and separation, unbelief and doubt, being closed to the move of God, lack of repentance and godly sorrow. Pharaoh was hard-hearted and was referred to as the great dragon (Ezekiel 29:3-5).

6. *[32]He maketh a path to shine after him; One would think the deep to be hoary.*
—Job 41:32

RESPONSE:
"He leaves a trail behind him."

A trail of misery, broken lives, and mass destruction. The path of pride leads to shame and destruction.

WHY IS LEVIATHAN SO PROUD?

7. *His scales are his pride, shut up together as with a close seal. One is so*

*near to another, that no air can come
between them.*
—Job 41:15-16

RESPONSE:
"His scales are his pride."
He has shielded himself with other spirits. To be delivered from Leviathan, the scales of the shield-demons must be removed.

WHAT ARE THE SCALES?

1. **Rejection**
2. **Lust**
3. **Hurt**
4. **Insecurity**
5. **Shame**
6. **Fear**
7. **Self-righteousness**
8. **Religious Spirits**
9. **Unforgiveness**

These scales are so tightly knitted together that the Spirit of God cannot flow. Demons draw strength by linking together. And if the Spirit of

God can't flow, you can't flow in the Spirit of God.Humility is the only way to defeat the Leviathan.

I humbled my soul with fasting; and my prayer returned into mine own bosom.

—Psalm 35:13

Fasting humbles the soul. We cannot defeat Leviathan in our own strength. It takes the power of God to crush and defeat him.

Conclusion

Leviathan is the spirit of pride. It is manifested through a sense of not needing to submit to anyone, including God. Leviathan dishonors covenants; he will not pray; he is stubborn, and he is hard-hearted. He leaves a trail of broken lives and mass destruction behind him, thus, leading to shame as declared in the scripture (Proverbs 11:2). This spirit is comprised of a legion of other spirits, including, rejection, lust, hurt, insecurity, and several others. Leviathan can be defeated through humility, fasting, and prayer. Also through the consisten- cy in keeping a clean heart before God, and asking for grace to sustain oneself from this spirit are other means of staying clear of this horrific force.

****

LESSON REVIEW

1. What is a leviathan?

2. What does the spirit of Leviathan do in times of prayer?

3. Name two of Leviathan's characteristics.

4. What does the statement "strength in his neck" suggest.

5. Name the eight scales of Leviathan.

6. What humbles the soul?

Scripture References:

Isaiah 27:1
Job 41:1-10, 30-34, 18-19, 22, 24, 15-16
James 3:5-6
1 Samuel 15:23
Psalm 35:13
Proverbs 11:2

The Day I Got Set Free

My Diary of Deliverance

The weapons of our warfare are not carnal, but mighty through God to the pulling down of strongholds. (1 Cor. 10:4)

Date: _____

- ☐ Monday
- ☐ Tuesday
- ☐ Wednesday
- ☐ Thursday
- ☐ Friday
- ☐ Saturday
- ☐ Sunday

**If two of you shall agree on earth as touching any thing that they shall ask, it shall be done for them. (Matthew 18:19)

Today Lord I set myself in agreement with Bishop George Bloomer and the mighty prayer warriors of Bethel Family Worship Center that this yoke will be destroyed in my life, in Jesus' name. Amen

_____

_____

_____

_____

LESSON 15: The Spirit of Pride

Personal Notes:

_____

_____

_____

_____

_____

_____

_____

_____

_____

_____

_____

_____

_____

_____

_____

_____

_____

_____

_____

_____

_____

_____

_____

_____

_____

_____

_____

_____

_____

_____

_____

_____

_____

_____

_____

_____

_____

_____

LESSON 15: The Spirit of Pride

_____

_____

_____

_____

_____

_____

_____

_____

_____

_____

_____

_____

_____

_____

_____

_____

_____

_____

_____

_____

LESSON

THE POWER OF WORSHIP

O come, let us sing unto the Lord: let us make a joyful noise to the rock of our salvation. O come, let us worship and bow down: let us kneel before the Lord our maker. —Ps. 95:1,6

INTRODUCTION

One of the most powerful, yet unsuspecting ways to break the spirit of oppression is through worship. Worship is powerful because it ministers to God. Worship is our opportunity to spend intimate time with the Lord, and even prostrate ourselves before Him in adoration and reverence. It goes beyond praise, which we many times use as a form of celebration for the good works that God has done.

> **PRAISE:**
> Hebrew: *Barak* - to bless
> *Shabach* - to address; to pacify

While it is equally important to praise God as it is to worship Him, worship requires relationship with Him. One must oftentimes have history with the Lord, and have a testimony that testifies of His miraculous working power in order to enter into the most Holy place of inexplicable worship. It's also worship, many times, that is required to repel the unmerciful attacks of Lucifer.

Believers must understand that every attack is not from the devil. Some attacks are allowed by God to build faith and perfect character, and even provoke an individual to his or her next level of ministry. Some attacks are merely preparation for more gruesome attacks that are ahead. It is worship, however, that allows an individual to overcome the attacks, preventing the attacks from overcoming them.

Remember, it was God who gave Satan the idea to attack Job (Job 1:8). The hand of God is upon His servants and Satan can not do anything, except he is granted permission by God. The good news, however, is that God will not allow you to be tempted (or attacked by the enemy) beyond that which you are able to bear (1 Corinthians 10:13).

Prayer

Lord Jesus,

We thank You for the privilege of being able to enter into Your very throne room to worship You. We thank You that when we worship, evil forces must flee from our lives. It is a result of the power of Your presence. Let this same presence be resident within us. Thank You. Amen.

LESSON

AN EVIL SPIRIT FROM THE LORD TROUBLES SAUL

Worship: to honor or reverence as a divine being or supernatural power; also, an act of expressing such reverence.

Greek: *latreuo* - to minister to God
proskuneo - to prostrate oneself.

But the Spirit of the LORD departed from Saul, and an evil spirit from the LORD troubled him.
And Saul's servants said unto him, Behold now, an evil spirit from God troubleth thee.
—1 Samuel 16:14,15

Saul's servants knew about God; so they inquired of their king to give them permission to free him of this evil spirit. They knew that the evil spirit was from the Lord and they knew that it would take a special servant of the Lord to be used as a vessel to make this spirit flee.

Let our Lord now command thy servants, which are before thee, to seek out a man, who is a cunning player on an harp: and it shall come to pass, when the evil spirit from God is

*upon thee, that he shall play with his
hand, and thou shalt be well.*
—1 Samuel 16:16

Saul's servants had much information and
were always well-equipped with knowledge on
how to supply the needs of the king. Yes, they
knew how to call on the god of wood, stone
and of fire, but they also knew how to call on
the Living God and how to get a prayer
answered by Him in times of trouble.

*And Saul said unto his servants,
Provide me now a man that can play
well, and bring him to me.*
—1 Samuel 16:17

Saul knew that this was a job that could only
be carried out by a God greater than any man-
made images.

*Then answered one of the servants,
and said, Behold, I have seen a son
of Jesse the Bethlehemite, that is
cunning in playing, and a mighty
valiant man, and a man of war, and
prudent in matters, and a comely
person, and the Lord is with him.*
—1 Samuel 16:18

As the story goes, Saul sends for David to play
the harp, and the evil spirit departs.

And it came to pass, when the evil spirit from God was upon Saul, that David took a harp, and played with his hand: so Saul was refreshed and was well, and the evil spirit departed from him.

—1 Samuel 16:23

The irony of the story, however, is that the evil spirit returns again to Saul in 1 Samuel 18:10-12.

And it came to pass on the morrow, that the evil spirit from God came upon Saul, and he prophesied in the midst of the house: and David played with his hand, as at other times: and there was a javelin in Saul's hand.
And Saul cast the javelin; for he said, I will smite David even to the wall with it. And David avoided out of his presence twice.
And Saul was afraid of David, because the Lord was with him, and was departed from Saul.

—1 Samuel 18:10-12

Many people rejoice over freedom, only to find themselves again cracking the door to receive once more, the bondage they before time fled.

WHY DIDN'T DAVID BECOME OPPRESSED?

Despite Saul's continual bouts with oppression, however, David *behaved himself wisely in all his ways; and the Lord was with him* (1 Sam. 18:14). Because David remained strong and did not succumb to the oppressive spirits that continued to haunt Saul, the Lord was with David and did not depart from him, as he did with Saul. David remained focused, in spite of Saul's murderous attempts.

Some of us are anointed to achieve certain tasks, but are killed simply because we succumb to the oppressive forces that are being transferred to us by people who hate us or are jealous of us. As a result, we succumb to whatever the oppressed individual feels, negating what God has said about us instead. We become the recipients of a demonic transfer.

Conclusion

In the preceding passage, Saul knows that he needs David's gift of **worship** in order to be delivered from this evil spirit, yet Saul is so jealous of David that he is willing to kill that which holds the answer to his deliverance. But because David understands the weapons of warfare and the power of worship, he is able to avoid the javelin twice and preserve his life.

Worship, especially private worship with God, will unveil the plans and devices of Lucifer. Worship will exalt you above every attempt and every attack. Worship is your secret weapon, and if you show God your weapon, He will build you an even stronger weapon to combat the artillery of Lucifer.

LESSON REVIEW

1. List the two Hebrew words for *praise*, and their meanings.

2. List the two Greek words for *worship*, and their meanings.

3. Worship, many times, is required to _____ the unmerciful _____ _____ of _____.

4. In the story of the oppression of King Saul, where did the evil spirit come from? What was the only thing that could repel this dark force? Why didn't David become oppressed by this spirit also?

Scripture References:

Psalm 95:1,6
Job 1:8
1 Corinthians 10:13
1 Samuel 16:14-18, 23; 18:10-12, 14

The Day I Got Set Free

My Diary of Deliverance

The weapons of our warfare are not carnal, but mighty through God to the pulling down of strongholds. (1 Cor. 10:4)

Date: _____

- ☐ Monday
- ☐ Tuesday
- ☐ Wednesday
- ☐ Thursday
- ☐ Friday
- ☐ Saturday
- ☐ Sunday

**If two of you shall agree on earth as touching any thing that they shall ask, it shall be done for them. (Matthew 18:19)

Today Lord I set myself in agreement with Bishop George Bloomer and the mighty prayer warriors of Bethel Family Worship Center that this yoke will be destroyed in my life, in Jesus' name. Amen

_____

_____

_____

_____

_____

Personal Notes:

_____

_____

_____

_____

_____

_____

_____

_____

_____

_____

_____

_____

_____

_____

_____

_____

_____

_____

_____

LESSON 16: The Power of Worship

_____

_____

_____

_____

_____

_____

_____

_____

_____

_____

_____

_____

_____

_____

_____

_____

_____

_____

_____

LESSON

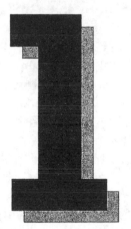

17

ANGELS AMONG US

And of the angels he saith, Who maketh his angels spirits, and his ministers a flame of fire.
—Hebrews 1:7,14

INTRODUCTION

The existence of angels is a fact, as their activities are accounted for throughout the Bible; Greek and Hebrew translations included. Angels are very real beings who definitely exist.

The word *angel* comes from the Greek word *angelos*; which means *messenger*. These unseen, intelligent beings are referred to as cherubim (Exodus 25:20), seraphim (Isaiah 6:2,6), and ministering spirits (Hebrews 1:14). They have been charged by God to keep us in all His ways (Psalm 91:11). They were the first to be created and are the highest in rank of all creation. However, being highest in rank does not make them equal to or above God. They are servants of the Most High and must never be worshipped. Their tasks include warring in the Spirit, delivering messages to and from God's throne, and protecting us, just to name a few. They are very active in our daily lives.

In studying angelology (the study of angels), one must look into its entire spectrum, which includes the doctrine of Satan and his army of evil forces; who are just as equally active in our lives. However, since we have already dealt with his kingdom to almost its fullest extent, we will only discuss the host of good angels who are busy carrying out the work of the Lord.

In this lesson, we will take a look at the creation and hierarchy of angels, the habitation of angels, the number of angels, the theory of angels having wings, and types of angels.

Prayer

Lord Jesus,

Thank You for this revelation knowledge of Your kingdom. No longer will we remain ignorant of the devices of the enemy, but we will know the make-up of the spirit world as a whole. The truths of these lessons will set us free in our minds and hearts, leaving worry and fear of the unknown behind. We know that You have created angels to war on our behalf, and to assist us in coming into the promises that You have ordained for us. We know that the enemy is trying to hinder our promise, but persistency and faith will fight off all the tactics that the enemy uses to block us from our destinies. Thank You for Your great love toward all mankind. Amen.

LESSON

Angel: an immortal, spiritual being attendant upon God. In medieval angelogy, one of nine order of spiritual beings: seraphim, cherubim, thrones, dominations or dominions, virtues, powers, principalities, archangels and angels.

HEBREW & GREEK WORDS AND MEANINGS
Hebrew Word: Mal'AK
Greek Word: Angelos
Translated: Angels, Messengers

THE CREATION OF ANGELS

Angels were the first to be created and are the highest in rank of all of God's creation.
Scholars assume that they were created simultaneously. They are different from mankind in that they make up a host, and not a race. Angels are a direct creation of God (this is why they are called *the sons of God* in scripture), whereas mankind is humanly reproduced (procreation). So mankind grows in number constantly, while the population of angels remains unchanged. Angels create a class of beings who are infinite, flawless, innumerable, and immortal. Unlike humans, they are unable to experience death or procreation. However, we humans are unlike angels in that we are able to experience redemption from sin through the blood of Jesus, and also experience the indwelling presence and baptism of the Holy

Spirit—an experience the angels long for: to have God inside of them.

There were certain angels, as discussed in Second Peter 2:4, Jude 6, Matthew 25:41, and Ezekiel 28:14-16, who transgressed the will and purpose of God for their existence. The story of their fall has been explored in Lessons Three and Four.

No one knows how long after the creation of angels that God created the physical universe, but it is told in Job 38:4-7 that the angels rejoiced over the completion of the earth's construction; thus indicating that they were present for at least the unveiling of God's newest architectural project. There is nothing said of other planets; only the earth is mentioned, thus revealing the object of God's love and concern—the earth and its inhabitants, who would soon be the recipients of His amazing grace.

THE CLASSIFICATION OF ANGELS

Various ranks/orders of angels are revealed in the scripture, thereby suggesting governmental authority among them. They are listed in Colossians 1:11-16 as:

1. Thrones (*thronoi*)
2. Dominions (*kuriotetes*)

3. Principalities (*archai*)
4. Authorities (*exousai*)
5. Powers (*dunameis*)

A definite hierarchy of angels is unknown, but we can safely assume that they are positioned in varying degrees of rank and station.

THE ABODE OF ANGELS

Their abode is generally understood as being with God in *heaven*. It is sometimes difficult to decipher the meaning of the word *heaven* in the scriptures. For instance, Genesis 1:1 states: *In the beginning God created the **heaven** and the earth.* However, in the Hebrew language, *heaven* is interpreted as *heavens*, which supports Paul's statement that he was caught up into *the third heavens* (2 Corinthians 12:2), thus implying a first and a second heaven.

The third heaven, to which Paul refers, is generally assumed to be the heaven where God reveals His glory. It's location is not revealed in the Bible but it is thought to be somewhere beyond the universe.

The heavens are believed to be as follows:

1. **The 1st heaven** - the sky; the atmosphere surrounding the earth; the airspace in

which birds and airplanes fly; the region that houses the clouds and the weather system; the firmament. (Matthew 8:20; 24:30; Genesis 7:11)

2. **The 2nd heaven** - the universe; outer space; the starry or stellar heavens; the cosmos; the region that houses the planets, galaxies, the solar system, moons, asteroids, stars, and other heavenly bodies. (Genesis 1:16; 26:4; Psalms 19:1)

3. **The 3rd heaven** - the heaven in which God and His host of heavenly angels reside; the heavenly city; the heaven of the redeemed; the heaven of God's glory. (Revelation 4:1-4)

Angels are thus clothed according to their residence and also to accommodate their spirit form.

Do Angels Have Wings?

It is believed that angels have wings because the scripture repeatedly tells us of the wings of the cherubim (1 Kings 6:24, 27; 8:6-7; 2 Chronicles 3:11-13; 5:7-8) and seraphim (Isaiah 6:2,6). Although many of these scriptures refer to sculptures of these creatures, it is believed that the sculptures are an exact replica of their appearance in heaven, as God is the One who instructed Solomon to make them (2 Chronicles 3:3).

When trying to decipher whether or not any other classes of angels have wings, it is hard to comprehend because there are only a few references that describe flying as their method of transportation (Daniel 9:21; Revelation 14:6). Another supporting factor of this theory is the swiftness with which they perform the commands of God.

Winged angels are generally accepted by the world's population due to the images that have been so prevalent in literature and the arts for so many centuries. However, the scriptures only support the theory of wings for the cherubim and the seraphim, and not the other classes of angels. It is only *suggested* that the other classes of angels (thrones, dominations, virtues, powers, archangels, principalities, and angels) have wings; and if this is so, the types and sizes of their wings are unknown to mankind.

ANGELS IN ACTION: WATCHING OVER US

*For he shall give his angels charge
over thee, to keep thee in all thy ways.*
—Psalms 91:11

Who maketh his angels spirits; his ministers a flaming fire:
—Psalms 104:4

Bless ye the LORD, all ye his hosts; ye ministers of his, that do his pleasure. Bless the LORD, all his works in all places of his dominion: bless the LORD, O my soul.
—Psalms 103:20-21

ANGELS MINISTERING TO MANKIND

1. Angels witnessed the promise of Abraham's seed (a son).	Gen. 18:1-14
2. As Christ was ascending, angels announced His return.	Acts 1:8-11
3. An angel became an adversary against Balaam.	Numbers 22:22
4. An angel instructs Joseph and Mary to flee into Egypt.	Matt. 2:13-15
5. An angel declares the resurrection of Jesus.	Luke 24:1-7
6. Angels came and ministered unto Jesus after he endured temptation.	Matthew 4:11
7. Angel sent to protect Daniel while he was in the lion's den.	Daniel 6:22
8. Angels participate in the giving of the law.	Galatians 3:19
9. Angel attends to Elijah.	1 Kings 19:5,7

10. Angels climb up and down Jacob's ladder.	Genesis 28:12
11. Angels hasten Lot to flee the city.	Genesis 19:15
12. Cherubim guard the tree of Life.	Genesis 3:24
13. An angel announces Jesus' birth.	Luke 2:9-14
14. An angel assures Joseph of God's purpose of the virgin birth of Jesus.	Matt. 1:18-25
15. An angel announces the birth of Jesus to Mary.	Luke 1:26-38
16. An angel announces the birth of the John the Baptist to Zacharias.	Luke 1:11-25
17. An angel smote 185,000 people in the camp of Assyrians.	2 Kings 19:35

THE ANGEL OF THE LORD

When referring to "the angel of the Lord" throughout scripture, this mysterious God-sent messenger can be identified in several situations as God Himself. Theologians and Bible scholars argue that this being was Jesus Christ present in the Old Testament. This messenger appeared to people who would not have been able to see the True and Living God and yet live. He can be found with a sword of judgement in several Bible stories. It is also believed that in not every instance is the angel of God really Jesus. Some instances clearly show a being that does not operate on its own accord, and in others it is more than obvious that the person is truly one of the Tri-Partite components of God.

THE ANGEL OF THE LORD IS SEEN APPEARING BEFORE SEVERAL PERSONS THROUGHOUT SCRIPTURE:

1. **Hagar** – *Genesis 16:7-13.* Hagar ran away because her mistress had dealt with her harshly. The angel of the Lord told her that he would multiply her seed exceedingly. Is there an angel who gives life? Only God Almighty has the power to give life (Job 33:4; 1 Timothy 6:13), as well as His equal counterparts within the Godhead: the Son (John 5:21) and the Holy Spirit (2 Corinthians 3:6; John 6:63). This was not just any angel.

   Genesis 21:17. She was sent away from her home. She and her baby were destitute – without food or water – in the middle of the wilderness of Beersheba; so she hid her son under a bush and waited for him to die. The angel of the Lord called to her, but in this instance, he mentioned that God had heard her child crying. So, we can safely assume that in this instance, he is not God.

2. **Abraham** – *Genesis 22:11-19.* Abraham is about to sacrifice his only son in obedience to the request of God. The angel of the Lord tells him to stop. He then says to Abraham, *By myself have I sworn, saith the LORD...*(verse16), clearly identifying himself as Lord.

   Genesis 18:1-33. Translated into English as *Lord* in this passage, but originally referring to the angel of the Lord.

3. **Eliezer** – *Genesis 24:7,40.*

4. **Jacob** – *Genesis 31:11-13.* Jacob had been mistreated by his father-in-law, Laban. He had a dream concerning the matter, in which the angel of the Lord spoke to him and said, *...for I have seen all that Laban doeth unto thee. I am the God of Bethel...* (verses 12,13). Again, he announces that he is God.

5. **Moses** – *Exodus 3:2-6.* The angel of the Lord appeared to Moses in a burning bush.

6. **Children of Israel** – *Exodus 13:21,22; 14:19.* While in the wilderness, a pillar of cloud led the children of Israel by day, and a pillar of fire led them by night. Chapter 13 of the book of Exodus tells us that the Lord was in these pillars. However, in chapter

14 we are told that the angel of the Lord was in these pillars. So who was in the pillars? Was it the angel of the Lord or was it the Lord? Or are these two people the same? **Think about it!**

Exodus 23:20-23. Judges 2:1-4 – The angel of the Lord speaks to the children of Israel as if he were God, repeating statements that were previously made by God Himself.

7. **Balaam** – *Numbers 22:22-35.* King Balak asked Balaam to join him in cursing the people of God. God was angry with Balaam, and the angel of the Lord stood in judgment with a sword drawn in hand. The angel spoke to Balaam and told him the very same words that God Himself had spoken a little earlier. Is this angel the same as God?

8. **Joshua** – *Joshua 5:13-15.* He announces himself to Joshua as *the captain of the host of the Lord* (verse 14). Joshua falls down and worships him. He tells Joshua to remove his shoes because the ground is holy. However, angels are not to be worshipped. In Revelation 22:8, the angel told John not to worship him, but to worship God only. So, the angel in Joshua 5 was clearly an equal counterpart with God.

Judges 6:11-24 – Gideon has an encounter with the angel of the Lord. The scripture keeps alternating between the angel of the Lord and the Lord as if it were one in the same person.

Judges 2:1-4 – The angel of the Lord speaks to the children of Israel as if he were God, repeating statements that were previously made by God Himself.

9. **David** – *1 Chronicles 21:16-18, 20, 27, 30; 2 Samuel 24:16-18.* In this instance, it is clear that God is instructing this angel on what to do. The angel is not acting out of his own power. There is no question about it. This is a messenger of God.

10. **Zechariah** – *Zechariah 1:11,12.* This is also an instance where the angel is not equivalent to God. This angel asks God about Jerusalem and Judah, whereas if he were equivalent with God, he would already know the fate of these two cities.

The angel of the Lord, when presented in the instances of being God, is all-powerful, able to give revelation, able to deliver, able to destroy, and able to forgive sins. The theory of his connection to Jesus was derived from John 1:1, 14, and also Colossians 1:16-19, which state that everything was formed by Jesus, and in Jesus, before the beginning; thus making Him the pre-incarnate Word who was with God at the creation of the world.

GIANTS

In Genesis 6:1-5, there is a story told of giants who once inhabited the earth. They were a mixed breed—a people of human and angelic form. The sons of God, or angels (whether good or bad is not discussed although some presuppose that this passage refers to fallen angels), noticed the beauty of the daughters of the men on the earth; so they took brides for themselves. The women, in turn, bare children, (They bare only male children. The scripture never mentions any "mighty women.") who then grew to be giants. One would have thought that this was not a natural phenomenon and would have ceased all ungodly activities, but the scripture says that giants were in the earth, and that the wickedness of man was great in the earth. When scripture says "in the earth," it means throughout, not designated to a certain region; so these activities must have been quite prevalent in order for it to be throughout the earth. So God became very angry, and decided to destroy all of mankind except for Noah and his family. This was because Noah walked with God, thereby fulfilling the scripture which says, *...Believe on the Lord Jesus Christ, and thou shalt be saved, and thy house* (Acts 16:31).

God had to honor His Word and save the family of Noah as well.

THREE MAJOR LEADERS OF HEAVEN'S HOSTS

1. **Michael** – Referred to in Daniel 10:13, 21; 12:1 as a "prince" who represents and defends Daniel's people – the Jews. Also referred to as the Archangel in Jude 9. He commands the angelic host of heaven in Revelation 12:7. His assignment appears to be to deliver God's people, especially the Jews, from the forces of darkness, and finally to evict these forces from the heavenlies; casting them down to the earth (Revelation 12:7-10). Michael also appears to have something to do with the resurrection of the dead. He is associated with the "resurrection" mentioned in Daniel Chapter Twelve. He also contended with the devil for the body of Moses, possibly for resurrection purposes (Jude 9). Also, his will be the "voice" of the archangel that will be heard when the "dead in Christ" shall rise (1 Thessalonians 4:16) for he is the only archangel that is mentioned in the scriptures.

2. **Gabriel** – Mentioned by name four times in the Bible. Twice mentioned in the book of Daniel, and twice more in the book of Luke.

He appears to be connected with the redemptive works of the Lord. He appeared to Daniel (Daniel 8:16; 9:21-27), informing him of Christ's first arrival. He notified Zacharias of the birth of the forerunner of the Messiah — John the Baptist. He later appeared to Mary and informed her of the birth of Jesus (Luke 1:19, 26, 27). He holds a prestigious position in heaven for he announced to Zacharias, *I am Gabriel that stand in the presence of God* (Luke 1:19).

3. **Lucifer** – Satan is discussed lastly, not because he is the least of these three, because in many aspects, he is the greatest; however, we do so because of his evil nature. He is the root of all evil in the universe. He once held the position of guardian or protector of the throne of God. The Bible declares that he was perfect in all his ways until iniquity was found in him. He had the audacity to exalt himself above his Master, consequently instituting a mutiny against the throne and the sovereignty of Almighty God. Because of his great prestige in heaven, he was able to influence and infect a throng of much lesser angels, consequently drawing them into a partnership in his unholy ambition. Thus, Lucifer himself, and the angels that sinned were cast down, losing their heavenly habitation, as well as their divine nature.

The heavens are populated with principalities of evil whom we are warned about in Ephesians 6:12. They are unclean in the sight of God according to Job 15:15; however, they will be cleansed so that the saints, the bride of Christ, and their groom, Christ Himself, may abide there safely during the Millennial reign of Christ.

Conclusion

Angels are the representatives of God, making significant announcements, warning of danger, aiding in destruction and judgment, warring in the spirit, and caring for God's people. Even fallen angels are known for their reverence of God and their obedience to His will (James 2:19). Good angels delight in praising the Lord continually, and a vast majority of them remain at His side awaiting their next command. In the immediate presence of God there are cherubim, seraphim, and living creatures/beings (Exodus 25:20, Isaiah 6:2; Ezekiel 1:5,6; Revelation 4:6). There are three major figures in the angelic world: Michael, Gabriel, and Lucifer (a.k.a. Satan). There is also the angel of the Lord who is likened unto Jesus because of his power in many of the instances in which he is seen. If you think back in your mind to a time when you thought or felt that

God was speaking to you, or a time when you were burdened, heavy-ladened, saddened by a death or an occasion, oppressed by a spirit and suddenly as if out of nowhere, the heaviness lifted and the joy came, you were probably touched by an angel.

****

LESSON REVIEW

1. Name the nine types of angels.

2. What does the word *angel* mean? What are the Greek and Hebrew words from which it is derived?

3. What other names are they commonly called in the scriptures?

4. Name the three heavens and describe them.

5. Who is normally referred to as the angel of the Lord?

6. What were giants? Give the scripture reference.

7. Name the three leaders of the angelic hosts.

8. Name some of the duties of angels.

Scripture References:

Hebrews 1:7,14
Colossians 1:111-17,19
Nehemiah 9:6
Psalms 148:1-5; 103:19-21; 19:1; 91:11; 104:4;
103:20-21
2 Peter 2:4
Jude 6,9
Matthew 25:41; 24:30; 1:18-25; 2:13-15; 4:11
Ezekiel 28:14-16; 1:5-6
Job 38:4-7; 33:4; 1 Timothy 6:13
Revelation 4:1-4,6; 22:8;12:7
2 Corinthians 12:2; 3:6
Daniel 9:21; 22; 8:16; 9:21-27
Numbers 22:22-35
1 Kings 19:15; 22:8
Galatians 3:19
2 Kings 19:35
Jeremiah 1:13-17
Luke 5:25; 1:2; 2:8,22; 24:1-7; 1:19,26,27
Acts 1:8-11;16:31
John 5:21; 6:63; 1:1,14
Genesis 1:1,16; 7:11; 26:4; 18:1-14; 3:24;
19:15; 28:12; 16:7-13; 22:11-19; 24:7-40;
Exodus 3:2-6; 13:21-22: 14:19; 23:20-23;
Judges 2:1-4
Joshua 5:13-13
1 Chronicles 21:16-18,20,27,30
2 Samuel 24:16-18
Zechariah 1:11-12

The Day I Got Set Free

My Diary of Deliverance

The weapons of our warfare are not carnal, but mighty through God to the pulling down of strongholds. (1 Cor. 10:4)

Date: _____

- ❑ Monday
- ❑ Tuesday
- ❑ Wednesday
- ❑ Thursday
- ❑ Friday
- ❑ Saturday
- ❑ Sunday

**If two of you shall agree on earth as touching any thing that they shall ask, it shall be done for them. (Matthew 18:19)

Today Lord I set myself in agreement with Bishop George Bloomer and the mighty prayer warriors of Bethel Family Worship Center that this yoke will be destroyed in my life, in Jesus' name. Amen

_____

_____

_____

_____

_____

Personal Notes:

_____

_____

_____

_____

_____

_____

_____

_____

_____

_____

_____

_____

_____

_____

_____

_____

_____

LESSON 17: Angels Among Us

_____

_____

_____

_____

_____

_____

_____

_____

_____

_____

_____

_____

_____

_____

_____

_____

_____

_____

_____

_____

LESSON

FROM ATOM TO ADAM

31And God saw everything that he had made, and, behold, it was very good. And the evening and the morning were the sixth day.

—Genesis 1:31

INTRODUCTION

It is important for believers to understand that the generational curses attached to their bloodlines did not originate with them. In this lesson, we will explore and confront some of the puzzling facets of the generational phenomenon, and reveal pertinent facts regarding the transition, which took place in mankind, causing curses to be inflicted upon him.

Prayer

Lord Jesus,

Thank You Lord for opening the eyes of my understanding and the courage to confront. Amen.

LESSON

Atom - smallest, indivisible particle of which all matter is formed; a unit of matter; the smallest unit of an element, consisting of a central, positively charged nucleus surrounded by a system of electrons and protons. Its entire structure is 10^{-8} centimeter and remains characteristically undivided in chemical reactions except for limited removal, transfer, or exchange of certain electrons. From Greek word *atomos* meaning *indivisible*, or *not cut.*

Adam - The first man, progenitor (forefather) of the human race. First man created by God in His own image (Genesis 1:27). He was created to have dominion over the earth (Genesis 1:26, 28).

Atomos - indivisible; uncut

Firmament - the expanse of the heavens; the sky

Atmosphere - 1. The mass or body of gases that surrounds the earth or any heavenly body. 2. Any surrounding element or influence. 3. The climatic condition of any place or region regarded as dependent on the air. 4. The general character or mood of one's environment; surrounding influence.

> *Atomos* (Greek) - vapor
> *Sphere* (Greek) - sparia

Cell - 1. The basic and smallest unit of an organization or movement 2. A portion of the atmosphere that behaves as a unit 3. A small, microscopic mass of protoplasm bounded externally by a semi-permeable membrane, usually including one or more nuclei and various other organelles with their products, capable alone or interacting with other cells of performing all the fundamental functions of life, and forming the smallest structural unit of living matter capable of functioning independently.

> [1] *In the beginning God created the heaven and the earth.*
>
> [2] *And the earth was without form, and void; and darkness was upon the face of the deep. And the Spirit of God moved upon the face of the waters.* [3] *And God said, Let there be light: and there was light.*
>
> [7] *And God made the firmament, and divided the waters which were under the firmament from the waters which were above the firmament: and it was so.*
>
> —Genesis 1:1-3,7

WHAT IS THE ATOM?

The atom is the smallest part of a chemical element that cannot take part in a chemical reaction without being permanently changed. Within the atom is also contained the nucleus (the atom's core), which is held together by a strong nuclear force. The nucleus houses protons, the positive particles, and neutrons, the negative particles. Both are essential to generate energy to the cells.

ADAM: THE ATOM-BUILDER FOR MANKIND

Creation is an act that only God can accomplish. Adam, being created in God's own image, was without sin; consequently, all that God created was good. Adam is described as the father and procreator of all mankind, while Eve is described as the mother of all living. When God created Adam, Adam became the nucleus (the beginning point; the originating forefather) for all mankind. The nucleus is a place of beginning to which additions are made, and is vital for growth and reproduction. From the nucleus of Adam, God generated the cell through electrical impulses, so that Eve could become a basic unit of living matter or tissue, called the "cell," to hold mankind together.

NUCLEAR FUSION: TWO BECOME AS ONE

Nuclear fusing is the splitting of the nuclei of atoms. When God created Adam, he also created Eve. ...*In the image of God created he him; male and female created he them* (Gen. 1:27). The nucleus is the seed that connects with the cells in order to produce after its own kind. The generated energy from the nucleus of Adam caused the cells outside of the nucleus wall to mutate. This transformation presents a vivid description of how molecular matter in its smallest form can exist without losing its chemical make-up.

"Mutation" indicates a change in form or of the development of characteristics that are not normal but are passed on by heredity. "Heredity" is none other than the passing on of certain characteristics from parent to offspring through chromosomes (from generation to generation).

Chromosomes: The tiny particles inside the cell the nucleus that contains the genes and carry the inherited characteristics within a generation.

The process of procreation began the process of begetting one's offspring. The prolific seed was to be fruitful, multiply, and reproduce after the very nature and character of God, Himself, but the curses came upon mankind because of disobedience.

THE FIRST NUCLEAR WARFARE

Nuclear warfare began when the serpent tempted Eve in the Garden of Eden (Genesis 3:1). In the natural study of nuclear warfare, the nuclear weapons are used against the enemy to create fallout. In chemical warfare, the chemical released is designed to destroy and disable the people. Our body chemistry is made up of elements and particles that enable us to function properly. While the chemical elements of nuclear weapons are carried by wind, the chemical elements of mankind are carried by the blood stream.

From the beginning of time, Satan sought to destroy mankind — to split into the nucleus (Adam), thus destroying both Adam and Eve. Remember, they were both created from the same Being on the same day!

So God created man in his own image,
in the image of God created he him;
male and female created he them.
                                    —Genesis 1:27

Satan's strategy became to "divide and conquer." The make-up of man is spirit, soul, and body. *The spirit of man*, as described in Proverbs 20:27...*is the candle of the Lord searching all the inward parts of the belly.* The spirit provides an entrance-way for God's light to bring spiritual understanding into our inner-most being.

According to scripture, the flesh and spirit war against each other continually. Therefore, after Satan deceived Eve by convincing her to obey the serpent's voice, the soul of man was not sure who to obey because beforetime, they were never forced to make choices. After Satan's deception, however, the flesh and spirit began to war one with the other.

Satan has always battled for the seed of mankind. His sole purpose was to prevent the coming of the Messiah to earth. Adam and Eve lost their dominion and became responsirble for what we describe today as generational curses.

THE CYCLE OF GENERATIONAL INIQUITIES

Many generational iniquities have been passed down from the fathers. Generation iniquities attach themselves to generations, holding families captive, unless the cycle is broken. Now let's take a closer look at generational sins that continue to rest in families and how to equip yourself with the ability to be released form the confines of Satan and his demons.

For years, many of us have witnessed our ancestors making statements such as, "You're just like you're Daddy (or Mother)." Usually, we're able to readily recognize similarities within families through certain characteristics and physical appearances. Generational iniquities, however, are oftentimes more difficult to recognize. Remember, children inherit both the good and sinful qualities of their parentage.

Satan will use subtle, yet incredibly forceful techniques to permeate the rights of believers to keep them bound. That is why the enemy attempts to make the things that small children do to appear cute. Normally, the dominant traits are hidden until the child begins to move into his or her teen to young adult years.

FROM ATOM TO ADAM TO ADAM

Although all of Adam's n eed was supplied in the Garden of Eden,he was a man; therefore his power was limited. Jesus gifted to us what the first Adam could not supply—redemption. Jesus (the 2nd Adam) came to redeem mankind from the curse (brought about by the first Adam) of the law (Galatians 3:13).

> 45And so it is written, THE FIRST MAN ADAM WAS MADE A LIVING SOUL; the last man Adam was made a quickening spirit.
> 46Howbeit that was not first which is spiritual, but that which is natural; and afterward that which is spiritual.
> 47The first man is of the earth, earthy: the second man is the Lord from heaven. —1 Corinthians 15:45-47

FLESH OF MY FLESH—BONE OF MY BONE

Think for a moment. Why did Jesus use a rib from Adam to create Eve as opposed to a leg, an arm, or a foot? The rib, of course, is a bone, and with the bone is contained marrow. From Adam, God used the bone marrow from Adam's rib so that the DNA from Adam would now be transferred to Eve. Likewise, this same DNA would be transferred to their children and their children's children, and so on.

Conclusion

Like the nucleus of an atom, which is essential for growth and reproduction, Adam is the beginning point of the human race. From the nucleus of Adam, God generated a cell (the basic unit of living matter), through electrical impulses, called Eve—she would house mankind within her womb. In creating Eve, God performed the first act of nuclear fusion by splitting the atom, Adam.

Nuclear warfare is a method of attack upon an enemy to create a fallout. Satan used this strategy in the Garden of Eden when he caused Adam and Eve to fall. Two wars continue to wage since that moment in the Garden of Eden, to the satisfaction of Satan:

1. The war of good against evil

2. The inward war of the spirit versus the flesh.

Since man's fall, sin has been passed down from generation to generation. The sins of the fathers rest upon the sons, thus causing generational iniquities.

We are made free from all sin through the redemptive work and blood of Jesus Christ (Romans 3:24-25). Sin no longer has dominion over us (Romans 6:14) if we do not yield to it. This goes along with the scripture that says, *Resist the devil, and he will flee from you* (James 4:7). God desires that we be liberated from the chains that the enemy will use to enslave us to sin. So resist, confess the Word, and be free in Jesus' name.

****

LESSON REVIEW

1. It is important for believers to understand that the _____ _____ attached to their bloodlines did not originate with _____.

2. What is an atom? What does it contain?

3. What part of the atom can Adam be compared to? Why?

4. What unit of matter is Eve compared to? Why?

5. What is heredity?

6. Why is nuclear fusion compared to the creation of man?

7. Name the first "nuclear warfare." What took place?

8. What two wars have been incessant since Satan tempted Eve in the Garden of Eden?

Scripture References:

Genesis 1:1-3,7,26-28,31; 3:1
Proverbs 20:27, Romans 3:24-25; 6:14
James 4:7

The Day I Got Set Free

My Diary of Deliverance

The weapons of our warfare are not carnal, but mighty through God to the pulling down of strongholds. (1 Cor. 10:4)

Date: _____

- ❑ Monday
- ❑ Tuesday
- ❑ Wednesday
- ❑ Thursday
- ❑ Friday
- ❑ Saturday
- ❑ Sunday

***If two of you shall agree on earth as touching any thing that they shall ask, it shall be done for them. (Matthew 18:19)*

Today Lord I set myself in agreement with Bishop George Bloomer and the mighty prayer warriors of Bethel Family Worship Center that this yoke will be destroyed in my life, in Jesus' name. Amen

_____

_____

_____

_____

_____

Personal Notes:

_____

_____

_____

_____

_____

_____

_____

_____

_____

_____

_____

_____

_____

_____

_____

_____

_____

_____

LESSON 18: From Atom to Adam

_____

_____

_____

_____

_____

_____

_____

_____

_____

_____

_____

_____

_____

_____

_____

_____

_____
_____
_____
_____
_____
_____
_____
_____
_____
_____
_____
_____
_____
_____
_____
_____
_____
_____
_____
_____